CW00796358

The
Back
Pocket
Mac
Book

The
Back
Pocket
Mac
Book

Tom Cuthbertson

Ten Speed Press
Berkeley, California

This book was written on a Macintosh Classic using MicrosoftWord 5.1 software. The graphic illustrations of computer parts, screens, and menus were created by the author using ScreenShot and SuperPaint. Design and page formatting were completed on Macintosh IIsi and IIci machines using Quark Xpress 3.11 software. The cartoon illustrations were scanned with a Hewlett Packard ScanJet IIc desktop scanner, tweaked in Photoshop, and imported to Quark Xpress for final page makeup. Completed art was supplied to the printer, Malloy Lithographing, in disk form on a SyQuest 44MB removable hard disk cartridge.

1☉
Ten Speed Press
P.O. Box 7123
Berkeley, CA 94707

Illustrations © 1993 by Ann Miya.
Text and cover design by Nancy Austin.

FIRST TEN SPEED PRESS PRINTING 1993

Library of Congress Cataloging-in-Publication Data

Cuthbertson, Tom
    The back pocket Mac book / by Tom Cuthbertson ;
illustrated by Ann Miya.
        Includes index.   p.   cm.
    ISBN 0-89815-527-4
    1. Macintosh (Computer)   I. Title.
QA76.8.M3C89   1993   92-36494
004.165—dc20   CIP

Printed in the United States of America

1 2 3 4 5 — 97 96 95 94 93

CONTENTS

For Colleen

ACKNOWLEDGMENTS

Thank you, Colleen, for being you and helping me be me while writing this book.

Thank you also to the following people, among many others, who helped to make this book. The artist Ann Miya, the editor Jackie Wan, and the designer Nancy Austin. Isaiah Carew, Cathy and Mike Boucher, Larry Allen, and the rest of the crew at Computerware of Capitola, California. Bill McDermott, my dear leprechaun friend of the MaCruzers users' group. Keri Walker, Doedy Hunter, Bob Olliver, and M. Lance Colvin at Apple, and all of the patient Apple support workers who have answered my endless questions. Laura Scribner of SeniorNet. David Mays and the rest of the folks at Dave's Computer Services in Santa Cruz. Howard Schneider of Canyon Consultants. And last but not least, my Kid Pix consultants, Chancy and Dylan.

INTRODUCTION

This little book is about using Macintosh computers.

When you first get a Macintosh, you can use the first couple of chapters of the book to put your Mac system together and learn the basic skills for using the mouse, the Mac desktop that you see on the screen, and the hard and floppy disks you use to store your work on.

After you have used your Mac for a while, you should still keep this book in a handy place for quick reference. If you have a compact Mac, stick it in the handle groove. If you have an LC, slip it in the space under the computer. If you have a modular Mac II or Quadra, stash the book on the back of the stand for the monitor. Whenever you need a reminder of how to do something, or whenever you have a little trouble doing something on the Mac, pull this little book out of its handy hiding spot and quickly find out what you need to know.

Of course, such a small book can't cover every possible problem you might have on the Mac, or every possible skill needed to use every feature of every application on the Mac. That's OK. Usually, if you are stuck or can't remember how to do something, you can find enough help in this book to get you going in the right direction. Then you can use your common sense, your imagination, and your knowledge of the basic Mac skills to keep going.

The Mac is a wonderful machine in that way; you don't HAVE to memorize hundreds of commands and codified command suffixes to make it do what you want. You can usually learn how to do new things intuitively. You learn as you use the Mac. It encourages you to explore, to try new variations of skills you already know, and build up computer knowledge and power on your own. This is much more satisfying than relying on others to teach you lists of commands.

But it isn't all easy. There are lots of new terms and concepts to master along the way, and there are lots of little tricks that can make your work easier if you can just remember how to do them. There are also a few pitfalls. You can lose things, have problems making things work, and get stuck in situations that seem impossible to get out of.

This book is written to help you learn the terms, tricks, and concepts you need to know to make the most of your Mac. It also has lots of good, clear advice on how to avoid the pitfalls and how to pick yourself and your Mac up and get going again if you fall into any of them.

The goal is to keep the smiles going, from the first smile of the Mac when you turn it on to your last smile when you see a fine piece of your work coming out of the printer. To achieve that goal, this book has cartoons, humorous examples, and personal anecdotes sprinkled through it. Each humorous piece carries a serious message, though, so you can learn as you enjoy.

So read on, and enjoy your Mac!

CHAPTER 1

Plugging In and Starting Up

This chapter is about putting the pieces of your Mac system together and turning the Mac on. It doesn't assume that you have ever used a Mac or any other kind of computer. In fact, if you know how to plug in a lamp and turn on the switch, you should be able to look at the pictures in this chapter and follow the directions just fine. If you can't figure out what a word means, just look it up in the Glossary at the end of the book. If you have some experience with computers, just skim over the material you are familiar with.

Checking the Parts

First get all the pieces of your Mac out and put them where you're going to be using the Mac. If you just bought a new Mac, take all of the pieces out of their boxes carefully, and find the instruction packets numbered 1, 2, and 3. Depending on what model of the Mac you have, you will have parts that look like those in one of the three illustrations below.

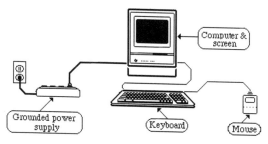

Illustration 1.1a: Compact Mac parts

Illustration 1.1b: Modular and PowerBook parts

The computer itself is a box with the little slot for floppy disks. On PowerBooks and portables, the computer, screen, and everything else are all in one unit. On compact Macs like the Classic, the screen and the computer are both in the same box. Whether it is attached to the screen or not, the computer should always sit on a flat, stable surface while you use it.

Turn the computer so the back is toward you for plugging-in purposes. You'll see a row of sockets or "ports" across the back of the computer, with a row of little pictures or "icons" above the ports, to help you figure out what plugs in where.

The monitor is the screen, and on all models except compacts and PowerBooks it is a separate unit. When you have everything plugged in and ready to go, the monitor should wind up on or near the computer, with no glaring lights or windows facing it or facing you while you look at it.

The keyboard is the thing you type on. The mouse is the little box with a squarish button on it and a ball under it; you may have a trackball or a stylus and pad instead of a mouse. The keyboard has two little round sockets on it. The mouse has a plug at the end of its cord; notice that the plug and the sockets all have icons that look like this:

You may have some other parts for your Mac, such as a little microphone, or a phono-plug adapter for input from a stereo, or some other peripheral devices such as a printer, a scanner, or network cables.

Check your packing list to make sure you have all the parts for your Mac system. Contact the dealer immediately if something is missing.

Setting Things Up

If you have a new Mac and you have all the instruction packets, get out packet #1, open it, and use the *Setting Up* booklet to set up your Mac. If you don't have any instructions for your Mac, use the following summary.

To prepare your Mac system for use, first make sure the computer is off. On most Macs other than PowerBooks and portables, the On/Off switch is on the back of the computer near the right side or the left side. It looks like a fat version of a wall switch for a light, except that instead of saying "ON" and "OFF" it has a 1 on the top and an 0 on the bottom. The 1 stands for ON and the 0 stands for Off; that's in binary talk.

Illustration 1.2: On/Off switch in Off position

Unless you are a computer nut you may not know the binary meanings of zero and one, but that's OK; just remember that the computer is off when the 0 is pushed in, as shown.

On PowerBooks and portable Macs, there is no On/Off switch. Just don't press any keys on the thing, and it will stay switched off.

When your Mac is switched off, plug in the power cord. Do this even on a PowerBook or portable, if you have a place to plug it in; the batteries are really only for short-term use while you are in transit. To plug in, push the socket end of the cord into the three-pronged socket on the back of the computer and plug the other end into a grounded power supply, such as the power strip shown in Illustration 1.1a. Make sure the power strip is properly grounded, and if you can manage it, get a power strip with surge protection; this will save your Mac from the ups and downs of electrical current that can damage its brain and wipe out its memory.

Once the power cord is plugged in, connect anything else that needs to be plugged into the Mac. If you have a modular Mac with a separate monitor, plug in its power cord and connect its cable to the port (socket) on the back of the computer that has an icon like a television screen. Unless the monitor is huge or the computer is an upright model, you can usually place the monitor on top of the computer. If the computer is sitting on your work desk and the monitor is sitting on top of the computer, it will be at about eye level, which is just where you want it. To minimize the effects of the monitor's electromagnetic field (extremely low frequency or ELF emissions), place it at least 30 inches away from your face. Nobody knows for sure how bad ELF emissions are, but the evidence so far indicates that they don't do us any good.

On all Macs but PowerBooks and portables, connect the keyboard to the computer, then connect the mouse to the keyboard, using the cables with the little round plugs on the end, and the sockets with the ADB icon. If the cable plugs have a flat side or an arrow on one side, make sure the flat side or arrow is up when you plug them into the computer.

Illustration 1.3: Mouse cable plug-in, with ADB icon

You can plug the keyboard cable into either end of the keyboard, and plug the mouse into the other end. If you are right-handed, plug the mouse into the right end of the keyboard. If you're left-handed, do it the other way around. Trackballs and stylus pointers connect just like the mouse.

For you Mac users who are accustomed to a mouse but have just bought a PowerBook, you can plug a mouse into your PowerBook so you don't have to learn to use the trackball. But if you are new to the Mac and have gotten a PowerBook, try to master the trackball. It is much more convenient to carry around, and you don't have to find room to drive a mouse around when you're using your Mac.

Additional Plug-ins

You may have other things you need to plug into your Mac before you turn it on. Although the manufacturers of all of these items insist that it is perfectly simple to connect them to your Mac, it can get a bit complex figuring out where all the cables and plugs go. Just follow these guidelines and the instructions that came with the device, and you should be able to get along without too many tangles.

SCSI DEVICES

A SCSI device is an extra piece of computer equipment that plugs into the SCSI (Small Computer System Interface, and pronounced "SKUH-zee") port. If you have an external hard disk drive and/or a scanner (a thing that can read text or graphics and translate them into data files for your Mac), read its instructions to find out which socket (or "port") the cable plugs into, and plug it in. Most external hard disk drives and scanners plug into the SCSI port. Mac people call them SCSI drives and SCSI scanners.

SCSI drives are not as simple as the hard drives that are built into your Mac. After you plug in a SCSI drive or other SCSI device, make sure you give it a unique ID number between 1 and 6. You usually do this by turning a little thumb-wheel or dial on the back of the SCSI drive case. Make sure your SCSI device is properly terminated, too; you need to add a terminator to the end of the cable on many hard drives. (This terminator, which often looks like a sort of plug-socket thingie, tells your Mac that the SCSI drive is at the end of the line; some SCSI drives have built-in terminators, but if there is no terminator, signals from the Mac try to keep going past the SCSI drive, looking for other devices, and they get lost; if you connect several SCSI devices in a chain, make sure only the last device has a terminator.) Also, make SURE you have an adequate cable; big, fast, fancy SCSI drives and high-resolution scanners are VERY sensitive to background "noise" due to static electricity coming through the cable. See the drive's instructions or contact a qualified technician for help with these critical SCSI setup tasks. Don't turn on the SCSI drive or the Mac until you are SURE you have the ID number and the terminator set up properly, and a first-class cable. You can have major file destruction problems if you start using a Mac with an improperly set up SCSI drive.

MONITORS

If you have a special color or large-screen monitor, you probably have to install an expansion card, then plug the special monitor into the socket on that card. See the instructions that came with your monitor and expansion card for help, or contact a qualified technician; this kind of plug-in is something that only needs to be done once, and it can be tricky, so get professional help if you have any doubts.

SOUND

If your Mac comes with a microphone for sound input, plug it into the port with the microphone icon. If you want to get sound input from a stereo or something, find the phono-plug adapter that was supplied with your Mac (it's a little Y of cable with a single plug and two sockets for phono jacks) and plug it into the microphone port, then plug the stereo's output jacks into the two sockets of the adapter.

PRINTER

If you have a printer, plug its cable or the AppleTalk cable for it into the port with the printer icon above it, unless its instructions tell you to plug it into the modem port (the one with the telephone icon). See page 116 for more info on setting up a printer.

NETWORK

If you have an AppleTalk or Ethernet network, the cable usually connects to the printer port, too. See your network administrator or someone who is familiar with your network to learn any special tips and tricks about using it.

MODEM

If you have a modem and expect to use it during the current session on the Mac, plug the cable for it into the modem port for your Mac.

Turning the Mac On

Once you have set up your Mac system, turn the computer and screen around and place them so the ports on the back of the computer are away from you, and the screen is facing you, at least 30 inches from your face (see the "Setting Up" section in this chapter for details). All you have to do is push in the 1 at the top of the On/Off switch to start the Mac up. If you have an external SCSI drive or other SCSI devices connected to your SCSI port, as explained in "Additional Plug-ins," make sure you turn them on before you start the Mac, so the Mac will recognize the SCSI devices as it starts, and put their icons on the desktop for you to use.

On most modular Mac models, once you have turned the Mac on for the first time, you can turn it off and on by pressing  a large key at the top of the keyboard; this key has a left-pointing triangle on it. If your modular Mac doesn't have this key, look for a small, square power-on key at the upper right corner of the keyboard. You can continue to use the On/Off switch at the back of the computer, but the preferred way of turning the Mac on is with the key on the keyboard.

What You See at Startup

When you turn your Mac on, it makes a beep noise, or it strikes a nice musical chord (C major) if it's one of the more advanced models. Then the screen lights up, and soon a little smiling Mac icon appears. It goes away and a message box appears, with the words, "Welcome to Macintosh." If your Mac is fast and your system software is relatively simple, you may see the smiling Mac and the Welcome box for only a few seconds. If you have an old Mac Plus and you're running System 7 with a bunch of custom software added, on the other hand, it will take some time to get through the startup sequence. You may see some little icons in the lower left corner of the screen as the startup sequence goes on; these icons show that you have some extensions added to your system software.

If you have any problem with startup, such as no beep, or an X or ? or sad Mac icon instead of the happy Mac, see Chapter 8; if the suggestions there don't help, see a good troubleshooting guide for help, such as *The Macintosh Bible,* or the *Macintosh Reference.* Or just go see a qualified Apple technician; it's important to get the Mac set up so it starts properly. If you have a very simple Mac with no hard drive, you will see the ? icon for sure; all you have to do in this case is insert a floppy disk with

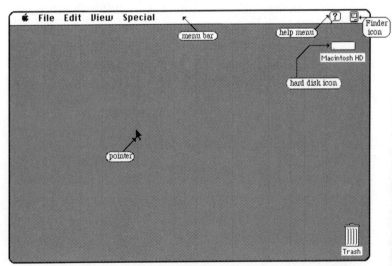

Illustration 1.4: Desktop on System 7

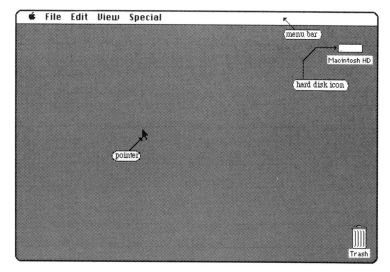

Illustration 1.5: Desktop on System 6.7 or earlier

the system software on it; the happy Mac should appear, then the Welcome box.

At the end of the Mac startup sequence the Welcome box goes away and the desktop appears. It looks something like either Illustration 1.4 or 1.5.

The System 7 desktop has a question mark help balloon and the Finder icon (the picture of a little Mac) in the upper right corner. Some earlier system software may show the Finder icon, but the question mark balloon is only in System 7 or later.

If you see a System 7 desktop that has the help balloon, but only three menus other than the one (File, Edit, and Special), and two big folder-like windows (one for Applications, one for Documents), then your Mac has At Ease installed. It is very simple to use; you just click either the button of the application you want to open in the Applications folder, or the button of the document you want to open in the Documents folder. See the "Clicking" section in Chapter 2 for hints on how to do it. Although At Ease makes life on the Mac very simple, there are usually severe limits on what you can name, move, or delete when using At Ease. See the primary user or administrator of your Mac system to find out what these limits are.

Whew; there's a bunch of new terms coming up all at once. We better define them clearly, right here at the start.

LEARNING ABOUT THE DESKTOP AND THE FINDER

The desktop is your working area on the Mac's screen. It is made up of the menu bar and the background area of the screen below the menu bar. You see all icons and other stuff ON the desktop. The Finder is the software that shows you the desktop and all the other stuff on it. That's why people say you are "in" the Finder when you are looking at the desktop.

If you are running System 7 or later, you see an icon for the Finder in the upper right corner of the screen when you are looking at the desktop, as shown in Illustration 1.4, so you

know who's running the show. You also see the help balloon icon (the one with the question mark) in the Finder. Look at your Mac's screen again; if you see the Help balloon, you are in luck; your Mac is running System 7, the text and examples in this book apply to you.

If your Mac is running an earlier version of the system software, and you don't see that tell-tale question-mark-in-a-balloon icon, as in Illustration 1.5, then you will notice that some of the explanations and procedures in this book don't work quite the way you expect on your Mac. Most of the differences are just in the look of things; the Mac works basically the same way on either the old system software or the new system software. You can still use the ideas and examples in this book, but you just have to adapt things somewhat. If you can afford to upgrade your Mac and use the latest system software, do so. System 7 requires a more powerful Mac than the earlier system software, but it is well worth the upgrade. System 7 makes it *sooo* easy to organize, find, and use things on your Mac.

For help with installing system software or updating to the latest version, it's best to see a qualified Mac technician or an experienced Mac user to make sure you set up the system software correctly and don't undo any custom set-ups that you have with your current system software.

CHAPTER **2**

How to Do the Basic Stuff

This chapter is the nitty-gritty of this book. It teaches you the basic things you need to know in order to use your Mac. You can work through it like a mini-tutorial; you start by learning to do things with the mouse, then you learn about all the things on the desktop and how to use them. The desktop, remember, is the area of the screen you work in — the menu bar at the top of the screen and the background below the menu bar where all the icons and windows appear.

Most of the lessons in this chapter are also covered in the Macintosh Basics tour that you get on a disk when you buy a new Mac. If you can dig out your Macintosh Basics disk, start

up your Mac with it in the floppy disk drive and take the tour it offers (for pointers on putting a floppy disk into the Mac, see page 30). The only trouble with this tour is that it requires you to stop and wait quite often, while it takes control of your Mac and shows you things in great and somewhat tedious detail. But if you can be patient with it, and just remember to keep clicking the little right arrow when you want to go on to the next step, the Macintosh Basics tour can be a very good supplement to the tutorial in the first part of this chapter, to help you learn and practice the basics of desktop technique.

Once you know your way around the desktop, you can use the other sections of this chapter to learn about using floppy disks, dealing with applications (the tools you use for your particular work on the Mac), and working with text, which you'll probably have to do no matter what kind of work you do. There is also a section on stopping work and shutting the Mac down.

Mouse and Menu Basics

The mouse is your key to the power of the Mac. All you have to do is master a few simple actions with it, then learn to use it with the Mac's menus, and you can quickly master any application that works on any Macintosh. So take your time and learn each mouse action correctly. For practice, you can use the Macintosh Basics disk, or just get a graphics application such as Kid Pix and play around with it for awhile; you'll probably find that your skill at using the mouse improves very quickly, without any great effort on your part.

Although the mouse is the key to the Mac's power, you can't neglect the keyboard completely. If you have not had any experience typing, you should buy a little program that helps you learn, like Mavis Beacon Typing. Many things you do on the Mac involve text, and you will also pick up keyboard shortcuts that speed your work, if you can type well.

POINTING WITH THE MOUSE

To point at something on the desktop, you move the mouse, holding it with your thumb and other fingers, but leaving your index finger floating over the button, as shown in Illustration 2.1.

Illustration 2.1: Moving the pointer with the mouse

Don't twist the mouse as you move it; keep the cable pointing away from you. A twisted mouse makes for bizarre pointer movements.

Practice moving the pointer from one object to another on the desktop. Place the *tip* of the pointer arrow directly on top of it. The tip of the pointer is its "hot spot." You'll know you're getting good at mouse control when you can quickly shift the pointer from the trash can to the Finder icon (it looks like a little Mac; if you don't see it, you're using an earlier version of the software, as explained at the end of Chapter 1) and then to the , without having to do a lot of twiddling around in each of the corners of the screen.

If the mouse seems to make the pointer move much too fast or much too slow, see page 83 for instructions on controlling mouse speed.

If the mouse moves the pointer to the edge of the screen, the pointer stops there, even if the mouse keeps moving. You don't have to worry about losing the pointer. It may quiver at the edge of the screen, but that's just its way of begging you to move the mouse back.

If the mouse moves off the edge of the table or mouse pad, all you have to do is lift it and put it back in the middle of the pad or desk-space; the pointer does not move when the mouse is raised up in the air. Try this out; the concept takes some people awhile to get used to. If you are one of those people, take your time and make sure you are comfortable with how the mouse works before you go on. By the way, I suggest you get a mouse pad that is designed to work with your particular mouse; mouse pads are easy to keep clean and therefore they make it easy to keep your mouse clean and smooth-running. If you do a lot of mousing, like for illustration work, get a Mouse Mitt or a similar wrist-protector; these can help you avoid getting a sore wrist and carpal tunnel syndrome.

CLICKING OR SELECTING

You click things to select them so you can do things with them. To select an icon, you move the mouse so the tip of the pointer is on the icon, then you press and quickly release the mouse button. Don't move the mouse while you are clicking its button. In Mac books the terms *click, select,* and *highlight* are often used interchangeably.

There are tricks you can use to select many things at once, such as shift-clicking and dragging a selection rectangle; for information on these techniques, see "Fancy Selecting" in the 37

"Window Basics" section of this chapter.

Practice clicking the Trash icon (the picture of the trash can in the lower right corner of your screen; it's the place where you can throw things away) and the hard disk icon (it's the box in the upper right corner of your screen) alternately on

Illustration 2.2:
Clicking the mouse

your desktop (if you have no hard disk, click the icon of a floppy disk that's in the upper right corner of the screen). When an icon is selected, it becomes highlighted; the shades of it reverse, so the dark parts become light and the light parts become dark. It may take you several tries to select an icon; usually the problem is that the tip of the pointer is not on the icon. Practice until you can select the Trash and hard disk icons quickly and easily.

OPENING THINGS BY DOUBLE-CLICKING

You double-click icons and other things to open them. To double-click an icon, point at it, then hold the mouse still while you click the button twice in rapid succession.

Now, you may wonder what it means to *open* things. In

the case of a disk or folder icon, or the Trash can icon, open means to open the item's window so you can see what's inside it. It's like opening the cookie jar to see what kind of cookies are inside. That's the kind of opening we'll do in this exercise. But in the case of an application, open means to start up the thing, and to open a document means to start up the document's application if it isn't already open, and look at the information in the document itself. Whew. That little word open can mean some pretty big and complex things. But you'll learn about them all in due time. Let's just stick to the cookie-jar level of opening for right now. OK?

Practice opening the Trash icon and the hard disk icon on your desktop. Windows appear for the two icons. When you get the trash and hard disk windows open, look at the stuff in each window. The hard disk window should have some folders in it (the icons look like little manila folders), but the Trash window may be empty. You haven't thrown anything into it yet.

Notice that the last window you open (called the active window) has a bunch of horizontal lines across the top, in the title bar. Notice also that the pointer sometimes turns into a little watch icon after you double-click something and before the thing opens; this is just the Mac's way of telling you to hang on for a second or two. When the watch is showing, the Mac is working as fast as it can to open the item you double-clicked.

If you try to double-click an icon and it becomes highlighted, but moves a bit instead of opening, the problem is that you moved the mouse between the two clicks.

If you press the mouse button twice and the icon becomes highlighted, but doesn't move and doesn't open, you are waiting too long between clicks. Try to double-click quicker. If that doesn't work, you may have to slow down the mouse's double-click speed. See page 83 for help with this.

Illustration 2.3: Double-clicking

CLOSING WINDOWS

To close an open window so it goes away and all you see is the icon, click in the close box, which is in the upper left corner of the window, at the left end of the title bar.

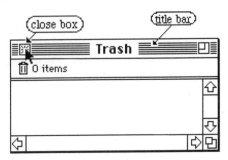

Illustration 2.4: Clicking in Trash window's close box

For more information on closing, see the "Basics of Stopping Work" section later in this chapter.

Close both the trash and hard disk windows, then double-click the trash and hard disk icons to open the windows again. Practice the opening and closing routine until you can do it easily. When you are done practicing, leave the hard disk window open—it's the window you need to use most often on the Mac.

DRAGGING

Dragging is how you move things around on the desktop and in windows. To drag an icon, point at it, press the mouse button and hold it down, then move the mouse in the direction you need to move the icon. You see a dotted outline of the icon moving across the screen. When the outline is where you want the icon, release the mouse button. Presto; the icon appears there. To drag a window, you put the pointer in the title bar (at the top of the window, where the title is) and drag it.

Try dragging the Trash can around on the desktop. Then open the Trash window. Drag the window until it covers up the Trash can, then close the window; the Trash can reappears. When you're done, drag the Trash can back to its corner; that's the best place for it, out of the way of windows. If you have dragged the hard disk icon out of its upper right corner, drag it back there, so you can find it easily, too.

CHOOSING COMMANDS FROM MENUS

One way to tell the Mac what to do is to choose commands from menus. They call them "pull-down" menus because you pull them down from the top of the screen like window shades. The titles of the pull-down menus appear in the menu bar across the top of the screen. To choose a command, point at the title of a menu (File, or Edit, for instance), press and hold down the mouse button, drag down through the commands to the one you want, then release the mouse button to choose the command. Notice that a highlighted bar moves down through the commands as you drag the arrow down, and when you release the mouse button, the command that is highlighted at that moment is the one the Mac obeys.

For example, here's how to use a menu command to open the Trash window. Select the Trash icon, then point at the word "File" in the menu bar, press the mouse button and hold it down while you drag the highlight down to the word **Open.** Release the mouse button while the word **Open** is still selected.

The Trash window opens; choosing **Open** from the File menu does the same thing as double-clicking the Trash icon. Most of the time it is quicker to double-click something to open it.

Commands that are not usable at the moment appear in gray

or dimmed text, like **Print** and **Close Window** in Illustration 2.5. To make a command usable, you have to be in a situation where it can be used. For example, you have to have a window open on the desktop in order to make the **Close Window** command usable. Now that you have the Trash window open, pull down the File menu again and choose **Close Window.** Notice that you can't choose **Open** when the Trash window is already open.

One further note about choosing commands; use only one command at a time. Sometimes, after you choose a command, you may see a little watch or a rolling beach ball icon in place of your pointer. These icons indicate that the Mac is busy carrying out your command. Don't try to choose a new command while the Mac is at work. It won't work, and it may actually cause a crash. See Chapter 8 for what to do in the case of a crash.

File	
New Folder	⌘N
Open	⌘O
Print	⌘P
Close Window	⌘W
Get Info	⌘I
Sharing...	
Duplicate	⌘D
Make Alias	
Put Away	⌘Y
Find...	⌘F
Find Again	⌘G
Page Setup...	
Print Desktop...	

**Illustration 2.5:
Choosing Open
from the File menu**

USING THE TRASH CAN

OK, you have pointed to the Trash can, moved it, opened it, and closed it. You must be wondering what the Trash can is for. If you need to get rid of something on your desktop, you drag it to the trash. The Trash can gets wider when you do it. To completely delete things you have thrown in the Trash can, you choose **Empty Trash** from the Special menu. Don't empty the Trash unless you are sure you don't need the things in there. If you ever decide you want something you have thrown in the Trash, all you have to do is open the Trash window and drag the item back out again. If you ever want to retrieve something you have emptied out of the trash, you have to have special tools and a little luck; see "You Lost a Document in the Trash" in Chapter 8 for details.

MENU BROWSING

On the Mac there is often a tricky quick way to do a thing, and a slower but easier way to do the same thing. Choosing a command from a menu is a good example. It may be a bit slow, but you don't have to remember anything to make it work. If you ever have trouble remembering how to do something quickly on the Mac, you can just point at the menu bar, press the mouse button and hold it down, then move the mouse to the

check your trash before dumping it!

left and right to see all the menus. Keep the pointer up at the top of the screen, so you don't highlight any of the commands while you browse. When you see the command you want, drag the highlight down to it and release the mouse button.

USING COMMAND (⌘) KEY SHORTCUTS

Many commands have keyboard shortcuts you can use so you don't have to pull down a menu with the mouse and drag the highlight down to the command. To use a shortcut, first you hold down the ⌘ key (that's the key with the little flower on it; on some keyboards, the key has an on it, too), then press and release the letter that is designated for the command. Then release the ⌘ key. It's much like using the Shift key to type an upper case letter. Usually the designated key is the first letter of the command. For example, you can choose the command **Open** by holding down the ⌘ key and pressing O. In this book, I put a hyphen between the ⌘ and the letter you press for a shortcut. For example, the shortcut for **Open** is ⌘-O; the shortcut for **Close Window** is ⌘-W. People who are fast typists will love ⌘ key shortcuts; they save a lot of time and jumping back and forth to the mouse. But if you are ever unsure of a command or its shortcut, remember that all you need to do is go menu browsing with the mouse; the shortcuts are listed right next to the commands. For additional info on what each command does, see the short reference in Chapter 3.

Window Basics

Once you can do the mouse and menu moves above, you're ready to go to work. All work you do on the Mac is done in windows. Here is a description of the parts of a window and what you can do with them. You can play around with each of the window parts in the list below, with the exception of the scroll bar. That requires a more complete explanation; see "Making a scrollable window and scrolling" on page 24.

LEARNING THE PARTS OF WINDOWS

1. **TITLE BAR:** The horizontal bar at the top of a window that shows the name of the window. When the window is active,

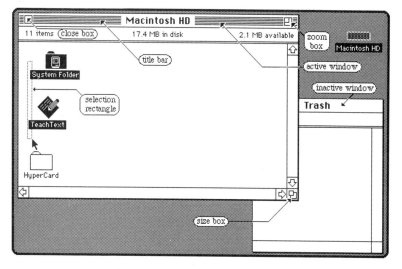

Illustration 2.6: Labeled windows

horizontal lines appear in the title bar. You drag the title bar of a window to move the whole window.

2. CLOSE BOX: The little empty square at the left end of the title bar; click in it and the window closes.

3. ZOOM BOX: A little box-in-a-box at the right end of the title bar. If you click it once, the window zooms to a new, optimum size (either filling the screen to display as many icons as possible, or to a shrink-to-fit size that displays all icons). Click the zoom box again to return the window to its previous size. If you hold down the option key and click the zoom box, it will fill the whole screen.

4. SIZE BOX: A box with two little overlapping boxes inside it, in the lower right corner of most windows. You drag the size box toward the center of the window to shrink it. To expand the window, drag the size box away from the window's center. It's like zooming, but you have more control.

5. SCROLL BAR, BOX, AND ARROWS: Scroll bars appear along the right side and/or bottom of a window if there is too much stuff in the window to show it all at once. For a description of how to use the box and arrows, see "Making a scrollable window and scrolling" on the next page.

SWITCHING WINDOW-TO-WINDOW

Once you begin doing serious work on your Mac, you'll probably have several windows open on the desktop at once. The active window is always on top. To switch from looking at the stuff in the active window to looking at stuff in an inactive window that is partly hidden by the active one, just click anyplace in the inactive window. If you can't see any part of the inactive window, just shrink or drag the active one to one side, to show at least a corner of the other window. Then click on that corner.

If you are working in several windows and need to switch back and forth between them, try to arrange them so a piece of each one sticks out beyond the others. For example, on a small-screen Mac, if you have three often-used windows, make them all the same size, about a half inch shorter than the width and height of the screen. Drag one window to the screen's top left corner, then put the next one down and to the right a bit, and the third in the lower right corner of the screen. That way, even if you switch from the first screen to the third and back to the first, you can still see the lower left and upper right corners of the middle window. This is called stacking the windows, and some applications do it for you automatically.

MAKING A SCROLLABLE WINDOW
AND SCROLLING

If you don't see scroll bars in any of your windows and want to try them out, do the following exercise. When the hard disk window is the active one (it has horizontal lines in its title bar) press the Option key on the keyboard, then click the zoom box to make the window fill the screen. Drag an icon or two down to the bottom of the window, so you have some icons at the top and some at the bottom. Then use the size box to shrink the window all the way up to the upper left corner of the desktop, so only one icon shows. Now you can play with the scroll bar, scroll box, and arrows on the right side of the screen. Click an arrow for a slight move up or down; hold an arrow

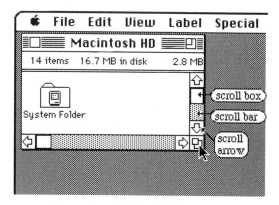

Illustration 2.7: Scrollable window

down to make the icons scroll slowly. Click in the gray part of
the bar to scroll a screen at a time, and drag the scroll box to
scroll to anyplace you want. Notice that the position of the
scroll box in the bar always tells you where you are within the
big picture; if you are looking at the folders near the top of the
whole available batch, the scroll box is near the top of the scroll
bar. If you are looking at folders near the bottom of the whole
batch, the scroll box is at the bottom of the scroll bar.

If a window is too small and you want to see more of the
whole batch of contents, click in the zoom box first, then scroll
the larger window. If you want to make the window small again
when you're done scrolling, just click the zoom box again.

Play around with the scroll bars for awhile. You have to
make things scroll several times using each of the arrows and
boxes before the scrolling principles become second nature to
you. It's worth taking some time to get good at it, because the
same scrolling principles work in windows for *all* text and
graphics documents. You'll be seeing those scroll bars all the
time on your Mac.

FANCY SELECTING AND
DE-SELECTING IN WINDOWS

Once you have mastered the basics of clicking and dragging,
there are some neat tricks you can use to select several things at
once in windows. To select a group of several icons that are
near each other, first place the pointer to one side of the whole
group, then press the button and hold it down while you drag a

dotted *selection rectangle* across them, as shown in Illustration 2.6. Notice that the rectangle doesn't have to enclose all the icons; all it has to do is touch part of each one. If you want to add one more icon to a group you have selected, shift-click it; point at the icon, press the Shift key and hold it down, then click the mouse button. Similarly, to de-select a single icon in a group you have selected, shift-click it. To de-select the whole group of selected icons, click somewhere else in the window.

File and Folder Basics

Most of the things you see on the desktop and in the window for your hard disk are icons for files or folders. These files and folders are the things you will deal with all the time as you do your daily work on the Mac.

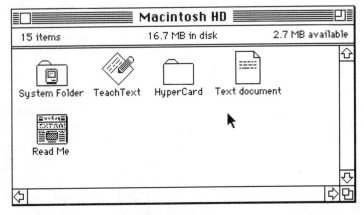

Illustration 2.8: Files and folders in a hard disk window

Files are the fundamental units of the stuff that's stored on any hard or floppy disk. Every file has a name. There are files that you make, called documents (in the Mac world) or data files (on other computers). There are also files that are tools, like your word processing program, and these are called applications or application programs; you make your documents with these applications. Then there are other files that work in the background to help things run smoothly on the Mac. These are called system files. Finally, there are some less familiar files that you'll learn about as you encounter them. The main files

TOOLS
(APPLICATIONS)

TeachText

make
PRODUCTS
(DOCUMENTS)

Document

for you to focus on now are the documents and the applications you use to make them.

Folders are containers for storing files. You divide up your documents and applications in folders so they don't all wind up in one oversized scrollable window. If you organize some folders inside others, you can make a nice, neat hierarchy. If you have ever used a DOS-based or UNIX-based computer system, you will remember seeing files organized into directories.

The System Folder is a special folder, usually found in your hard disk window; it contains all the files of system software and things that help the system software run your Mac the way you want. Don't open the System Folder and mess around with the files and folders inside it until you have had a good deal of experience using the Mac, and have learned what all the pieces of the system software do and how they do it. You can easily disable the Mac or bring it to a crashing halt by messing with the system software. Messing around in the System Folder is like messing around with the innards of your car's engine. If you like messing with the innards of things, see a complete manual on the Mac, such as *The Macintosh Bible,* and learn all about the workings of the System Folder and the Mac's system software. It isn't all that hard to learn about, if you put a little time and effort into it.

OK, enough of that heavy warning stuff. To see how files and folders work, do the following short exercise. You'll make your first folder, and start putting things in it.

First make sure the window for your hard drive is open and active. Double-click the hard disk icon if it isn't.

MAKING AND NAMING A FOLDER

Choose **New Folder** from the File menu. A folder appears in the hard disk window, with its name, "untitled folder," selected. Type the word "Applications" to give your new folder a name. Make a second folder by choosing **New Folder** again, and type in the name "Misc. Small Stuff." No matter what other folders you put on your hard disk, you'll probably want to have these two sooner or later, so you might as well make them now.

OPENING AND CLOSING A FOLDER

All you have to do to open a folder is double-click on the icon for it; a window for the folder will open, displaying its contents. To close the window for a folder, just click the close box. Try double-clicking the Applications folder; the window that opens is empty, because there is nothing in the folder yet. Click the Close box to close the Applications folder window. Note how it shrinks down into the folder's icon. Ain't that slick?

MOVING A FILE INTO A FOLDER

If you see the TeachText icon in your hard disk's window, drag the icon to the Applications folder, and when the folder becomes highlighted, release the mouse button. The TeachText icon disappears from the hard disk window. Now double-click the Applications folder icon again; you'll see the TeachText icon in the newly-opened window of the Applications folder. If you have some other applications, drag them into the Applications folder.

MOVING FOLDERS INTO A FOLDER

If you have a folder on your hard disk with an application in it, such as a HyperCard folder, or a Word 5 folder, you can drag the whole folder to the Applications folder, just as you dragged the single file, TeachText. Now, if the Applications folder window is closed, you can drag the application files and folders to the Applications folder icon. But if the Applications folder window is open, and it isn't covering up the hard disk window, you can drag the application files and folders from the hard disk window to the Applications folder window. Either way, the Mac just moves the files and folders right into that folder.

Get how it works? Good. This is the key to organizing things on the Mac. If the concepts aren't clear to you yet, do some more moving of files and folders around (like, move TeachText back to the hard disk window, then move a folder from the Applications folder to the hard disk, then move the file and folder back into the Applications folder). If you ever wonder what's inside a folder, just double-click it and the window for it will open. For more information on organizing things into a nice, neat hierarchy of folders, see the "Folders and Files" section of Chapter 5.

After you have worked with file and folder icons and folder windows for a few weeks or so, and have gotten really comfortable with the basic concepts, you can put the contents of any window in a list view, then move things from folder to folder, all inside the same window. That way, you don't have to keep opening and closing all those windows and moving them around so they don't cover each other up. For more information on working with list views, see the "View Menu" section of Chapter 3.

USING AN ALIAS FOR A FILE OR FOLDER

An alias is a stand-in for the icon of a file or folder. It's not a nickname; it's more like a substitute. The alias behaves like the original icon, but it hardly takes up any room. This saves space and lets you open files or folders without having to hunt for them. For example, you can leave a favorite application in your Applications folder, but put an alias for the icon on your menu, where you can get at it to open the application at any time. To make an alias for the application, find and select the icon for the application, then choose **Make Alias** from the File menu. The alias-icon appears. Note that the title is in italics. You can edit the name of the icon, but it will always be in italics so you can distinguish it from the original. Drag the alias icon to the Apple Menu Items folder in the System Folder. Presto, it appears in your menu. Choose it and the application opens. You can put aliases for much-used files or folders on the desktop or in your hard disk window, too. In fact, whenever you use any item a lot, just make an alias of it and put it on the desktop, in your hard disk window, or in the menu. Just remember, if you delete the original item, you must delete the alias, too.

Floppy Basics

A floppy disk or floppy, for short, is a little round plastic disk that can store software—applications or documents—for your Mac. The disk itself is flexible and floppy, but it is contained in a square hard plastic case with a metal door. You insert a floppy by sliding it into the disk drive slot, label side up, round hub down, and the metal door going in first. But first, you need to know if it is the right kind for your Mac. Then you can insert it and, if it is a brand new floppy, get it initialized so the Mac can copy things on and off it. Once you have the initialized floppy in your Mac, its icon will appear on the desktop. Then you can copy things to and from it. The sections that follow cover these points in detail. For some hints on protecting floppy disks and the data on them, see Tip #6 in Chapter 4.

LEARNING ABOUT 800K AND 1.4MB FLOPPIES

All floppies that fit into Mac floppy drives are the same size (3.5 inch) but some hold more software than others. Floppy disks are rated by how many kilobytes (K) or Megabytes (Mb) of data they can hold. A megabyte is equal to a thousand kilobytes. What is a kilobyte? A thousand bytes, or about a quarter page of text. So a floppy that holds 800K of data will hold a good-sized book full of text. A 1.4Mb floppy disk can hold

Illustration 2.9: 800K and 1.4Mb disks

about two short books worth of text. Graphics can use up much, much more storage area.

To tell the difference between an 800K floppy and a 1.4Mb floppy, look at the corners of the plastic case when the front of it is facing you, as shown in Illustration 2.9. The 800K floppy has one hole in the upper right corner. The 1.4Mb floppy has two holes, one in the upper right corner and one in the upper left corner. It also has a funny-looking symbol in the lower left corner, which is made out of the letters "H" and "D" pushed together. That stands for High Density.

If you have a late model Mac, with the standard SuperDrive that comes in all recent Macs, you can use either 800K or 1.4Mb floppy disks. If you have an older Mac, you can only use 800K floppies. If you work on some Macs that have SuperDrives and some that don't, you can have some nasty problems; see "The Mac Says a Disk is Unreadable" in Chapter 8.

INITIALIZING, OR GETTING A FLOPPY READY TO USE

Before your Mac can copy things on and off a brand new floppy disk, it has to set up a format on it, or initialize it, in Mac jargon. If you put a brand new floppy in your floppy disk drive, a little box, called a dialog box, appears on the screen, as shown in Illustration 2.10.

To get the floppy ready for use, just click the Initialize button, the rectangular space in the dialog box that has the word

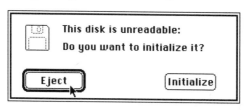

Illustration 2.10: Initialize dialog box

"Initialize" in it. For more information on dialog boxes, see "Saving Your Work" later in this chapter. If you are using an older Mac, the dialog box will have a "One-sided" and a "Two-sided" button. Click the Two-sided button unless you have a Mac that is older than a Mac Plus. Those rare old Macs can only read one side of a floppy.

If you ever see a dialog box like the one in Illustration 2.10 just after you have inserted a floppy that you *know* has stuff on it and should be readable, DON'T click Initialize or Two-sided. Click Eject, and when the Mac spits out the disk, go to "The Mac Says a Disk is Unreadable" in Chapter 8. If you initialize a floppy that has files and folders on it, the Mac erases all the stuff on the disk!

COPYING THINGS TO AND FROM FLOPPY DISKS

To copy a file or folder from your hard disk onto a floppy disk that has been initialized, first insert the floppy. Its icon appears on the desktop. Drag the icon of the item you want to copy from the hard disk window to the icon of the floppy. Or, if the window of the floppy disk is open and it isn't covering the hard disk window, you can drag your selected item from the hard disk window to the floppy's window.

To copy something from a floppy disk onto your hard disk, all you have to do is insert the floppy disk, open the window for it, and then drag the icon for the item you want to copy to the icon for the hard disk on the desktop. You can then move the item to the appropriate folder, as explained in "File and Folder Basics" in this chapter.

Notice that when you drag a file or folder from one disk to another, the item you drag does not disappear from its original place. The Mac leaves the original file or folder there and puts a copy on the other disk. This is different from dragging items from one folder to another. The difference can be summed up in this little rule of thumb:

Dragging items between folders MOVES them.
Dragging items between disks COPIES them.

The reason for this difference is that you can easily lose a file or folder by dragging it from your hard disk to a floppy, then losing the floppy. You can always find an item if it's just in another folder on your hard disk.

For information about moving files and folders from one floppy to another, see "Copying from one floppy disk to another" in Chapter 5.

Application Basics

Applications are software programs that come on floppy disks. You use them like tools to get things done on the Mac. This section tells how to pick good ones, install them, start them up, and then save and print the work you do in them. It also tells how to switch between different documents you are working on in an application, and how to switch between applications, too.

CHOOSING APPLICATIONS FOR YOUR WORK

Seek out and buy the best applications you can afford; any craftsperson can tell you that superior tools are worth every extra penny they cost.

For instance, to write things on the Mac, you need a good word processor application such as MacWrite, Microsoft Word, or WordPerfect. If you do financial reporting or forecasting, you need a good spreadsheet application such as Excel, Resolve, or Lotus 1-2-3. If you need to manage lots of information, you need a good database like FileMaker Pro or 4th Dimension. If you do business accounting, you need something like MYOB (Mind Your Own Business); for personal accounting, you can get a program like Quicken. If you are an artist or illustrator, you'll need a graphics application like MacDraw, Canvas, Painter, Freehand, or Adobe Illustrator. If you are a desktop publisher, you'll need something like PageMaker, QuarkXPress, or FrameMaker; for small projects, you might use Aldus Personal Press. There are many other good applications for specific needs, but make sure that the ones you get are known to be easy to use, reliable, well-supported, and compatible with your Mac's version of the system software. See magazines like *Macworld* or *MacUser* for reviews and compatibility reports.

If you are on a short budget and your Mac isn't one of the high-powered models, you might try one of the integrated packages of software, such as ClarisWorks (my fave by far), Microsoft Works, BeagleWorks, or Symantec GreatWorks. Each has its strong points, but none pretend to give you the power and flexibility you can have with individual applications for jobs such as word processing and illustration. I find the Works word processors painfully clumsy and limited, for example, but I write for a living. If you only need to write simple letters and make a simple advertising flyer now and then, an integrated application package might work just fine for you.

Whatever applications you decide to use, don't pirate them. Copying an application from another user is not only against the law, it is destructive to the whole Mac community; if good software programmers and resellers can't make any money because their products all get ripped off, they'll stop making and selling good software, and we'll all be up the creek without a paddle.

INSTALLING APPLICATIONS

To install an application you have bought, first lock the floppies by sliding the small tab on the back of the floppy case toward the edge of the case, so the little square door is open as shown in Illustration 4.2. Then insert the Program or Application disk (sometimes labeled Disk 1) in your Mac's floppy drive. A

Installer

window usually opens, showing an Installer icon. Double-click this icon to start the installer program. Then just follow the instructions on the screen to complete installation.

If you see a dialog box during installation that tells you to turn off your virus-detection software, do so; some installations can be ruined by watchdog virus-detection programs. To turn such programs off, you usually have to choose **Control Panels** from the menu, then open the control panel for the virus-detection program, then click the Off button. After closing the control panel, you usually have to restart your Mac to make sure the virus-detection program has turned off. When you have finished the installation, turn the virus-detection program back on and restart the Mac again.

If you have any other problems with installation, or your Mac does not have enough storage space or memory available to use an application, see a qualified technician or a complete Mac guide such as *The Macintosh Bible* for help. If your Mac is short of memory and you can afford to add some, by all means, go for it. You'll never regret adding memory. See Chapter 5 for details.

REGISTERING WITH APPLICATION MAKERS

After you have installed the software you need to do your work, you'll probably be itching to try everything out. Before you plunge in, though, take a few minutes to fill out the registration cards you got with your applications. Mail in the registration cards right now, so you don't forget.

Why bother? Because you get lots of free stuff. If you are a registered user of your Mac and its system software, for example, you get free over-the-phone help from Apple's customer service department; Apple support used to be pretty minimal, but it is quite good now, and a great free resource to have during your first weeks as a Mac user. You can usually get some free or cut-rate support from software makers, too, and you are always entitled to special rates for upgrades to new versions. The best software companies also send out free notices if they find bugs, and some even send free bug fixes.

Most registration forms also ask if you want to receive "supplementary information." This translates to junk mail in most cases, so I usually say no. If they don't say anything about it, I write a note at the bottom of the registration card, saying please don't put me on any advertiser's mailing lists, thank you.

STARTING WORK IN AN APPLICATION

You can go to work on the Mac in two ways; by opening an application and starting to work on a new document, or by opening a document that you have already made. This section covers both of these approaches.

When you are in the Finder and you are looking at files and folders in windows on the Mac's desktop, the most obvious way to start up an application and start working on a new document is to double-click the icon for the application. You may have to open an Applications folder or another folder that contains the application in order to see the application's icon. When you start the application from its icon, a blank, untitled window for a new document opens.

If you want to start work on a document you have already created, just double-click the icon for the document. The application starts if it was not already open, and the window for the chosen document opens.

If you have trouble finding either an application or a document you want to double-click, just choose **Find...** from the File menu in the Finder, and type in as much as you can remember of the name of the item you're looking for. Then click the Find button and let the Finder go get it for you. If you don't find the item on your first try with the **Find...** command, try **Find Again.** Ain't it slick? *That's* why they call it the Finder. For more hints on easy finding and opening of applications and documents, see page 140.

Once you have a new or old document's window open, you can begin work on it. You use the commands in the application's menus and the mouse to do your work. Refer to the application's manual if you do not understand how to use a particular command or feature it provides.

SAVING YOUR WORK

As soon as you have done some work in a document, either creating new material or editing stuff you did before, you should save your work. Saving is simply taking what the Mac is holding in its memory and writing it onto the hard disk. This protects your work. If you just leave it all in the Mac's memory, a sudden power surge or outage can wipe it all out. It doesn't happen often, but when it does happen, it can be a disaster. So save your work often, like ever 15 minutes or so.

To save your work, just choose **Save** from the File menu. You can also hold down the ⌘ key and press S. The first time you choose **Save** or press ⌘-S after you open a new document or any time you choose **Save as...** from the File menu, you see a dialog box that looks more or less like the ones in Illustration 2.11. A dialog box is a small window that appears on your Mac screen with things you can choose to do or not to do. You have

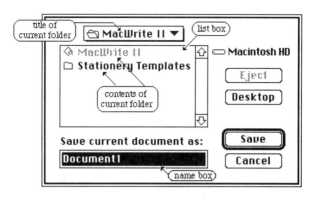

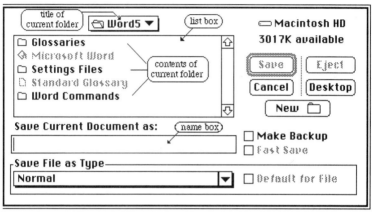

Illustration 2.11:
MacWrite II and Word Save as... dialog boxes

to make some choice or at least click a button, such as an OK or a Cancel button, to make the dialog box go away so you can go back to work.

Every application has its own particular style of Save dialog box; some are pretty simple, like the MacWrite II one, while others are or more complex, like the Word one. They all have a list box, which shows a list of the files and folders in your currently active folder (the Folder that the application or document you're working on is in) and a bunch of buttons. However, to do your basic save, you don't have to fiddle around with all those buttons and stuff. Just use the following short procedure.

To save a document right where you are, in the currently active folder, all you have to do is type a short but unique name for the document and click the Save button (some applications

like Word, as shown in Illustration 2.11, dim the Save button until you type in a name). Later, if you decide you want to put the document in another folder (leaving documents in the same folder with your applications can get messy), all you have to do is go to the Finder (click on the background or the hard disk icon outside your application's window), open the folder with the new document in it, then drag the document icon to the folder where you want to store it. If you aren't sure where you want to store it, you can put it in the hard disk window, then go to "Folder Hierarchy for File Storage" in Chapter 5 and learn how to make a sensible place to store new documents.

ADVANCED SAVING TECHNIQUES

To save your new document in a folder other than the current one with its contents in the list box, you have to choose **Save as...** from the File menu, then mess around with the list box and its title. You may want to skip these fancy saving techniques until you've had some experience on your Mac. The techniques do take a little practice to get good at, but don't worry, you can practice all you want in a Save dialog box, as long as you don't click that Save button until you are sure you're putting the new document in the folder where you want it. Even if you *do* click Save by accident and put the document in the wrong folder, it's no big deal to just go to the Finder and drag it out of the wrong folder into the right one. So when you feel comfortable with the Mac and the files and folders on your hard disk, jump right into the following procedures so you can save your work wherever you want it.

If you want to save the new document in a folder that appears in the list box, you double-click the folder's name (notice that only folder names show in dark text; names of files are dimmed because you can't put things inside them); the folder's name will then appear as the title and its contents will appear in the list box. You can click in the name box, type a name for your new document, then click the Save button.

If you want to put the new document in a folder that is somewhere else on your hard disk, you have to do some navigating. First pull down the menu formed by the title of the current folder (how about that; it is a menu; a pop-up menu, to be precise; don't ask me why they call it a pop-up menu when it actually pulls down; that's just the name programmers gave it when they invented it!) and choose the name of your hard disk from the menu. For example, if I were saving a TeachText document, and I was using the TeachText application in a TeachText folder inside the Applications folder, as shown in Illustration 2.12, I'd choose **Macintosh HD** from that pop-up menu. The name of the hard disk then appears as the title for the list box, and the folders and files on the hard disk appear in the list box. Double-click any folder you want to open. For example, if I wanted to put my new TeachText document in a folder such as Misc. Short Stuff, I'd select that folder name in the list box, then double-click that folder. When the title of the folder you want is at the top of the list box and its contents are listed, click in the name box, give your new document a name, then click the Save button. For example, I would click in the name box and name my document, "Teach-Text sample 1," then click the Save button.

If you want to put the new document on a different disk from your current hard disk, pull down the pop-up menu and choose Desktop,

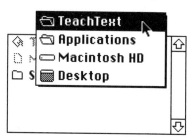

Illustration 2.12: List box pop-up in Save dialog box

down there at the bottom of the menu. The title of the list box becomes Desktop, and all available disks in drives connected to or in your Mac are listed. Click the drive you want, then double-click your way down into the folder where you want to store your document.

If you want to use a document as a template for many similar documents, such as form letters or invoices, you can save it as a Stationery document. Sometimes this option appears as an icon in the Save dialog box, or sometimes it is in a File Type menu, as at the bottom of the Word dialog box.

The above procedures cover most situations you'll run into when saving new documents. There are all kinds of fancy saving tricks that can be done with special pop-up menus and buttons like the ones shown in the Word dialog box, but I'll let you explore those on your own, with the help of your application's manuals.

PRINTING YOUR WORK

After you have saved a document, you can print out a hard (paper) copy of it. In most cases, it is pretty easy to print a document. If you have a printer hooked up to your Mac and ready to print, and you are looking at the document in its window, all you have to do is choose **Print** from the File menu and click the Print button in the dialog box that appears. Don't worry about all the other buttons and stuff in the window; you don't need them for most normal printing.

If you have an inkjet or laser printer, you'll be amazed the first time you see how nice your document looks when it comes out. THIS is why we use Macs instead of typewriters. The Mac even gives you a way to see what the document is going to look

Illustration 2.13: Print dialog box

like before you print it; in most applications you can choose a command such as **Preview, Print Preview,** or **Page View** from the File, View, or Page menu. A reduced view of the document appears on the screen, showing exactly how the text or graphics will line up on the printed page.

For information about hooking up a printer and setting things up so you can print, and for details about all the options you can use when printing documents, see Chapter 7.

SWITCHING BETWEEN OPEN DOCUMENTS

Most applications let you open more than one document at a time. If you have two documents open in one application, the easiest way to switch between them is to set up their windows so neither one completely covers the other; then you can click on the window of either document to make it the active one. Many applications also list the open documents in the File, View, or Window menu, so you can choose the one you want to have active; this is especially helpful if you have a small-screen Mac with lots of documents open. It's hard to stack all the windows so they don't cover each other up. Just remember to save your work in each document before you switch to another one; to save, choose **Save** from the File menu, or press ⌘-S.

SWITCHING BETWEEN OPEN APPLICATIONS AND THE FINDER

When you first work on the Mac, you'll probably want to do only one thing at a time. But when you have a bunch of experience and know how to use more than several applications, you may want to use a couple at the same time. If your Mac has enough RAM (memory) to run two or more different applications at once, such as a word processor and a graphics application, you can switch from one application to another, without having to quit either application. All you have to do is pull down the Application menu from the icon that is at the far right end of the menu bar and choose the new application you want to switch to.

You can also switch to the Finder (the thing that shows you windows with all the icons for files and folders) and back in the same way. For example, you can write a description of a new product in a word processor, then switch over to a drawing of it and work on that, and go back to the word processor to refine the description so it matches the drawing. If you can't remember where a file is that you want to work on, you can just switch over to the Finder and use **Find...** to hunt through all the folders for it, as explained in the "Starting work in an application" section earlier in this chapter. For details on how much RAM you need to run your applications, see Chapter 5.

If you have lots of windows open in two applications and you don't want the screen to be cluttered when you switch into the new one, just hold down the Option key as you choose the new application from the Application menu. This hides the windows of the old application and shows the windows of the new one. You can use the same trick to hide windows as you switch to the Finder and back. To return to the hidden windows, just choose the application (or **Finder**) from the Application menu; all of the hidden windows reappear.

If you only have a couple of windows open, one in one application and one in another, you can place the windows so neither covers the other completely, then simply click in the two windows to switch from one application to the other. You can also hold the Option key down as you click in a new window, in order to hide the old one.

Text (Word Processing) Basics

This means writing stuff on the Mac. Mac people don't call it typing, even though you use a keyboard. They call it working with text, or word processing. Whatever you do on the Mac, you'll probably spend some of your time working with text. The following techniques can be used in many different word processing applications, from TeachText (which you get free with your System Software from Apple), to MacWrite II, which costs about a hundred dollars or so, to Microsoft Word, which can cost three or four times as much as that. You can also use most of the simple techniques on the desktop when you name files and folders; names of files and folders are text, too, after all.

To start working in any word processing application, you can double-click its icon. The application opens and a window for a document appears on the screen, with a title at the top that says something like "Untitled" or "Document 1." There is lots of blank space in the window for you to fill with text. For other methods of getting started, see "Starting work in an application" earlier in this chapter.

ENTERING, CHANGING, DELETING AND MOVING TEXT

The following paragraphs tell how to get text onto the screen, how to change it, delete it, and move it. There is also a paragraph on undoing mistakes you make while working with text.

To enter text (to make words appear on the screen), you just type at the keyboard when you can see the insertion point. The insertion point is usually a blinking vertical line. If you have just opened a word processing application, the insertion point should be blinking near the upper left corner of the blank window. When you start hammering the keys, the words march across the screen behind the insertion point. If there are already words on the screen, you can place the insertion point wherever you see the I-beam instead of the normal pointer. Move the I-beam to the place where you want to enter text, click the mouse button, and when the insertion point appears, start typing. Notice

Illustration 2.14: Pointer, I-beam, Insertion point

that if you place the I-beam on a blank line or in the blank space at the end of a document, the insertion point appears at the left end of the blank line, or at the end of the last word at the end of the document.

To change or *edit* text you have typed, you must first select it. This works in all word processing programs, and it works in the Finder, too; you have to select the title of an icon before you can edit it. To select some text, move the I-beam to the beginning or end of the text and drag across it. When the text is highlighted (selected), you can type in whatever you want to replace it with; the Mac makes room for the new text if it is longer or shorter than the old text. To extend a selection, place the I-beam anyplace past the end of the selected block of text, then hold down the Shift key and click the mouse button. You can use the same technique to shorten a selection, shift-clicking inside the selected block of text. All this stuff works when you're editing text in the titles of files and folders on the desktop. Here's another handy trick for selecting text that works in most word processing applications; double-click on the first word of text you want to select, then shift-click to extend the selection to

the last whole word. This is often easier than dragging, which requires pretty accurate handling of the mouse or trackball.

To delete text you have typed, first select it, then press the backspace key. If you make a small mistake in a single word and see it right away, all you have to do is press the backspace key and backup over the mistaken word, then type the word correctly.

To move text, first select it, then choose **Cut** from the Edit menu. Move the I-beam to where you want to place the text, click the mouse button to place the insertion point, then choose **Paste** from the Edit menu. To copy text, use the same procedure, but choose **Copy** instead of **Cut**.

To correct a mistake in typing, deleting, cutting, copying, or pasting, just choose **Undo** from the Edit menu immediately after making the mistake. For example, if you select a large block of text that you want to copy, but then hit a single key by mistake, the block of text disappears and is replaced by the single letter. To bring back the missing text, just choose **Undo**.

FORMATTING WITH THE RULER

Use the Ruler at the top of the document window to set margins, indents, tabs, line spacing, and alignment of the text. If the ruler is not showing, look in either the View or Format menu for a **Ruler** or **Show Ruler** command. The ruler will look and work more or less like the Word ruler shown in Illustration 2.15. In some applications, some of the settings are made in menus or dialog boxes. TeachText has no ruler, unfortunately; it doesn't have ways to change text format much.

To change the alignment of the text from left-justified to centered, right-justified, or full-justified, click the button or box that shows the text aligned the way you want it.

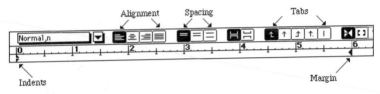

Illustration 2.15: Ruler for Microsoft Word

To change the line spacing, click the button with narrow, medium, or wide spacing. In typing terms, these usually correspond to single, 1 1/2, and double spacing. The two buttons to the right of the line spacing ones in the Word ruler shown in Illustration 2.15 are for spacing between paragraphs; most word processors do not have buttons like these because you can just hit Return an extra time to put a blank space between any two paragraphs.

To set a tab, drag the type of tab you want from the button to the position you want on the ruler. There are buttons for left-justified, centered, right-justified, and decimal tabs.

To set the indents and the right margin, just drag the triangles to where you want them. The top triangle on the left sets the first line indent for each paragraph.

Many word processors provide menu choices to change the font, size, and style of your text. To make any of these changes, select the text first, then choose the command from the appropriate menu. Try it; changing **fonts** and font sizes is a kick.

WHEN YOU'VE FINISHED YOUR TEXT DOCUMENT

After you have entered, edited, moved, and formatted the text of a document, you need to save your work. You may also want to print it out. These procedures are covered in "Application Basics," earlier in this chapter.

Basics of Stopping Work

These are the basic moves you do when you're finished with work. They include closing windows, quitting applications, shutting down the system software, and turning off the Mac and any external hard drives, printers, or other stuff.

To close a window when you are done working in it, choose **Close** from the File menu, or press ⌘-W (in most cases).

To quit working in an application, first choose **Save** from the File menu to save your work on any documents you have created or edited, then choose **Quit** from the File menu, or press ⌘-Q. The windows for that application's documents close and the application disappears from the Application menu. If no other applications are open, you go to the Finder. For more information on saving your work in an application, see "Saving and Backing Up" in Chapter 6.

If you forget to save your latest work when you close a window or quit an application, the Mac reminds you; just click Yes in the small dialog box that asks you if you want to save your changes to the document before closing.

To shut down the system software so you can turn your Mac off, first quit any applications you are using, then choose **Shut Down** from the Special menu. As the Mac shuts down, it checks to make sure you have saved your latest work; if you have forgotten, a box appears, asking if you want to save your changes. Click the Save button unless all of your most recent changes are mistakes. When the Mac has shut down its system software completely, the screen goes dark and a message box appears, telling you that it's now safe to turn the Macintosh off. Turn off the Mac when you see this box.

DO NOT turn off the Mac or unplug it without doing the shutdown procedure just explained. You should

Illustration 2.16:
Choosing Shut Down

take special care to make sure you never turn off or unplug the Mac while it is writing to or reading from a floppy or hard disk. You can lose all the information on the disk if you turn off the spinning drive. If you ever notice that the plug for your Mac is loose, don't adjust the plug until you have saved your work and shut down.

If you have an external SCSI hard drive, turn it off after you turn the Mac off. You can turn off printers, scanners, and other peripheral stuff either before or after you turn off the Mac.

Practice Makes Pleasure

To get good at using the mouse, the menus, and stuff like windows, and have fun in the process, I suggest you get Kid Pix, one of the most wonderful graphics applications ever created for the Macintosh, and one of the cheapest, too. Just follow the instructions in the super-easy Kid Pix manual and fool around for an hour or so. The concepts will sink in quickly, and you will soon become adept at things like dragging and double-clicking. You will also get at least one good chuckle and a couple of wows. If you can't afford a copy of Kid Pix, you can use the Macintosh Basics disk (start up your Mac with it in the floppy disk drive) and use it to practice all the basic Mac moves, but frankly, I think Kid Pix is a lot more fun.

CHAPTER 3

Menu Choices—
A Quick Reference

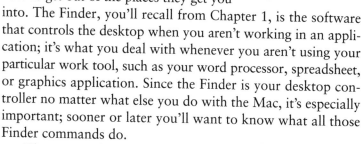

When you can do all the basic Mac moves, you can use this chapter as a little reference section, to remind you of what the different Finder menu commands do, and how to get out of the places they get you into. The Finder, you'll recall from Chapter 1, is the software that controls the desktop when you aren't working in an application; it's what you deal with whenever you aren't using your particular work tool, such as your word processor, spreadsheet, or graphics application. Since the Finder is your desktop controller no matter what else you do with the Mac, it's especially important; sooner or later you'll want to know what all those Finder commands do.

The menus that you see in the Finder let you do a wide variety of things, from opening a document to shutting down the Mac. Here are the choices, listed as they appear in the menus. For each choice, the result is described, accompanied by a way to get back to the situation before you made the choice. If a command is grayed or dimmed, that means it is not available at the moment. Often commands are dimmed because you have not selected anything for them to act on. For example, you have to choose a document to print before the **Print** command becomes available.

Keep in mind that ⌘ key shortcuts are listed to the right of the commands. For example, in the File menu, ⌘-O is the keyboard shortcut for **Open**; to use it, hold down the ⌘ key and press the O. Oh, it gives you such a feeling of power. And if you are a fast touch-typist, using the shortcuts can save you loads of time and effort; you'll hardly ever have to reach over for the mouse!

⚫ MENU

Gives you direct access to things at any time, whether you are in the Finder or in an application. You can put anything you want in the ⚫ menu, from utilities to applications, from files to folders, or aliases of any of them. The following list is just the stuff that Apple sends with your Mac. Illustration 3.1 shows a more or less standard, short ⚫ menu and also a sample of a highly built-up ⚫ menu, with hierarchical submenus such as those you can get with utilities like HAM or MenuChoice. For more information about building up and using the ⚫ menu, see "Adding customizing extensions and control panels" in Chapter 5.

ABOUT THIS MACINTOSH...: In the Finder, tells you how much RAM (Random Access Memory) you have in your Mac, how much RAM is not reserved at the moment, and how much each open application is using. For details, see page 93. In other applications, this option varies; usually it is About-the-application.

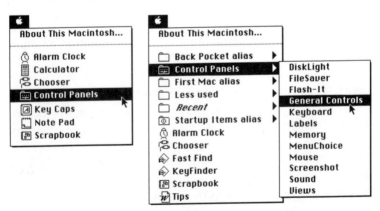

Illustration 3.1: ⚫ Menu; a short, stock version and a built-up, hot-rod, hierarchical version

ALARM CLOCK: Opens a little message box that tells you the time. Click the close box to make it go away.

CALCULATOR: Opens a little window that looks like a pocket calculator. Click the close box to make it go away.

CHOOSER: Opens a window that lets you choose what printer and what other network stuff you want to use. Click the close box to make it go away.

CONTROL PANELS: Opens a window that lets you choose which of the controls for your Mac (such as General Controls, Mouse speed, or Screen brightness) you want to adjust. Double-click a control icon to adjust the control. Click the close box to make the window go away. For more info on control panels, see "Using control panels to customize things" in Chapter 5.

KEY CAPS: Opens a window that shows the keyboard and the characters that each key creates in a given font. Click the close box to make the window go away.

NOTE PAD: Opens a small window where you can enter notes or other short text items. Click the close box to make the window go away.

SCRAPBOOK: Opens a window showing the first of a number of items stored for pasting into your work. Click the close box to make it go away.

FILE MENU

Has a lot of different purposes, from opening and closing things to setting up network connections.

NEW FOLDER: Creates a new folder in the active window and highlights the title so you can give the folder an appropriate name. To get rid of a folder, drag it to the trash.

OPEN: Opens a disk's window if a disk has been selected, opens a folder's window if a folder has been selected, opens (starts) an application if an application has been selected, opens a document in the correct application if a document has been selected. Double-clicking is a quicker way to open all these things. To close a disk or folder window, just click the close box. To

New Folder	⌘N
Open	⌘O
Print	⌘P
Close Window	⌘W
Get Info	⌘I
Sharing...	
Duplicate	⌘D
Make Alias	
Put Away	⌘Y
Find...	⌘F
Find Again	⌘G
Page Setup...	
Print Window...	

Illustration 3.2: File menu

quit an application, choose **Quit** from the File menu. To close a document, click the close box.

PRINT: Prints a selected document by opening the application that made the document, then printing from within that application. Not the standard way to print things. To get out of printing, click Cancel in the Print dialog box that appears. Then click the close box of the document's window to close it, or choose **Quit** from the File menu to quit the application.

CLOSE WINDOW: Closes the active window. To open it again double-click the icon the window shrank down into.

GET INFO: Opens a small window with a bunch of information about the selected file or folder. Useful for finding out things about applications, like how much memory is allotted to them. To close the Info window, click the close box.

SHARING...: Opens a sharing window for sharing selected files or folders on a network. If you don't want to share the selected item, just click the close box.

DUPLICATE: Makes a copy of the selected file or folder (and its contents). The copy appears in the same folder with the original, and *Copy of* is added to the original's title. If you don't want a copy, drag it to the trash.

MAKE ALIAS: Makes a copy of the icon of the selected file or folder. The alias has an italicized title. If you don't want the alias, drag it to the trash. For more on aliases, see "Using an alias for a file or folder" in the "File and Folder Basics" section of Chapter 2.

PUT AWAY: Puts selected file or folder icon that is on the desktop back in the folder on whatever disk it came from, OR ejects selected floppy disk from the disk drive. To get a file or folder icon back on the desktop, just open the window of the disk that contains it and drag it back to the desktop. To see an eject-ed disk's icon back on the desktop, insert the disk in the floppy drive again.

FIND...: Opens a dialog box that lets you specify the name of a file or folder you want to find. When you find the item, double-click it to open it. Click Cancel to close the dialog box.

FIND AGAIN: Finds another example of the last file or folder name you specified in the Find dialog box, and opens the window of the folder containing the found item so that it can be shown highlighted. Close the window to go back to where you were in the Finder.

PAGE SETUP...: Opens a dialog box that lets you make settings for your current printer, like paper size and orientation. Click Cancel to get out of the dialog box without changing any of the settings.

PRINT WINDOW...: Opens a dialog box that lets you specify how to print out a hard copy of the active window. Click Cancel to get out of the dialog box without printing anything.

EDIT MENU

Lists commands that help you edit text or graphics. You usual-ly do all editing in applications, such as word processors or graphics applications, but there are times when you can edit things on the desktop. For example, you can edit text in the titles of files and folders, and you can sometimes edit text in dialog boxes.

UNDO: Undoes the last editing you did, if possible. If you undo an action and then decide it wasn't a mistake after all, just choose **Undo** again, and the Mac will take the action again for you.

CUT: Removes any selected text or graphic and places it on the clipboard, a temporary storage place in the Mac's memory. You can use Paste to place the cut item somewhere else. To replace

Edit	
Undo	⌘Z
Cut	⌘H
Copy	⌘C
Paste	⌘U
Clear	
Select All	⌘A
Show Clipboard	

Illustration 3.3:
Edit menu

something you have cut, choose **Undo** before you do any other editing actions.

COPY: Places a copy of any selected text or graphic on the clipboard, the Mac's temporary storage place. You can then paste the copy repeatedly in other places in your work. To get rid of the copy on the clipboard, just cut or copy something else, or restart the Mac.

PASTE: Takes the last item you cut or copied onto the clipboard and places it at your current insertion point. You can paste an item as many times as you want; it stays in the clipboard until you turn the Mac off or Cut/Copy something else into the clipboard.

CLEAR: Removes selected text or graphic without placing it on the clipboard. To retrieve a cleared item, you must choose **Undo** from the Edit menu before you do anything else.

SELECT ALL: Highlights all appropriate material in the Active window. If you want to cut, copy, or clear the selected items, choose the appropriate command. Click in blank space to de-select the highlighted items. Beware of selecting things that are not visible in the window; use the scroll bars to check for stray selected items.

SHOW CLIPBOARD: Opens a window that displays the last item you cut or copied. Click the close box in the clipboard window to make it go away.

VIEW MENU

Gives you a choice of ways to display the items in the active window. The first two views show you pictures or icons for the items; the other views list the items in a sort of outline form; they are thus called "outline" or "list" views. To change from one icon view to another, choose the new view from the menu. To change from one list view to another, you can simply click right in the window on the type of view you want to see. For example, if you are looking at a view **by Name**, the "Name" heading will be underlined; click on the "Kind" heading to list the items by Kind and underline that heading.

View
- by Small Icon
- ✓by Icon
- by Name
- by Size
- by Kind
- by Date

Illustration 3.4:
View menu

BY SMALL ICON: Shows files and folders in miniature, with the names next to them, so you can put lots of them in a window, in rows or columns.

BY ICON: Shows files and folders as large, detailed icons with the names under them. You can arrange them in rows and columns, or stagger the icons so long names don't overlap.

BY NAME: Lists files and folders together, alphabetically, in outline view.

BY SIZE: Lists files and folders together, arranged by size, largest first, in outline view. To show sizes of folders, see the "Adjusting Views" section in Chapter 5.

BY KIND: Lists files and folders separately, in alphabetical order, in outline view.

BY LABEL: Lists files and folders together, ranked from Essential down to Project 2, depending on which label you assign to each item; see the "Label Menu" section below for details. On color Macs, the files with different labels have different colors. You don't see a column titled "Labels" in list views if the "Show Labels" option is not checked in the Views control panel. I never use labels (I name my folders and documents carefully, so they don't need labels); therefore my list views are less wide, allowing me to see the last modified time and date without scrolling, even on my puny Mac Classic screen. Brevity is a fine thing.

BY DATE: Lists files and folders together, ranked from newest (most recently modified) to oldest.

I usually keep my view in a **by Kind** listing, so I can get a clear notion of where stuff is in the hierarchy of folders. Other users prefer **by Name** list view. Use the view that suits you, but after you've been working on your Mac a while, try out the list views; they're really handy when you have lots of files and folders.

If you want to see what is inside a folder that is shown in a list view, just click the right-pointing triangle that is in the margin next to the folder's icon. The list expands, like a little outline, showing you what files and folders are in the selected folder. If you want to hide the contents of an expanded folder so you can save room to show other folders in the window, click the down-pointing triangle next to the icon of the expanded folder. This collapses the outline of the folder's contents so you can't see them.

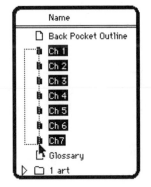

Illustration 3.5:
Selecting a group of
documents in a list view

When you are familiar with list views and have some experience with the expanded and collapsed outlines of folders, you can learn some shortcuts that speed up your work. For example, you can use a selection rectangle as shown in Illustration 3.5 to select a bunch of files all at once. To learn more shortcuts choose Finder Shortcuts from the Help menu and read the screen, "Working with outline views."

LABEL MENU

Lists different labels you can assign to files and folders to rank them and keep them in separate groups in list views. This is only needed if you have lots of files or folders with similar titles. The Label menu does not appear unless you choose to display labels in the Views control panel, as explained in Chapter 5. The labels appear in the menu listed by priority, from **Essential** through **Hot, In Progress,** and **Cool,** down to Project 2. This ranking order is not obvious when you first look at it. You can substitute clearer label names of your own by means of the Labels control panel. One drawback to labels is that you have to apply them to all the documents you make, including each new one, in order for them to be a viable organizing tool.

Illustration 3.6:
Label menu

SPECIAL MENU

Contains commands for basic Mac chores like cleaning up, emptying the trash, and shutting down for the day.

CLEAN UP WINDOW: In icon views, puts the icons in a more or less regular pattern in the active window. You may have to reposition an icon or two when the cleanup is done; the Mac doesn't always choose the most useful arrangement.

EMPTY TRASH: Removes all items you have thrown in the trash, unless they are locked or in use. You see a dialog box warning you how much stuff you are about to remove permanently. To bypass the warning box and delete even locked items, hold down the Option key as you choose **Empty Trash.**

EJECT DISK: Ejects the selected disk from the floppy drive and leaves a ghost icon behind. Use only for ejecting a floppy that you want to copy things to from another floppy (see page 99). For normal ejecting of floppy disks, choose **Put Away** from the File menu, or just drag the floppy's icon to the trash.

ERASE DISK: Whoa, this is a heavy one; it completely deletes everything on the selected disk, unless it is the current startup disk that the Mac is running off of. You see one of two little dialog boxes, depending on which size disk you are about to erase. If you are erasing a 1.4Mb HD disk, click the Initialize button. If you are erasing an 800K disk and want to keep using it as an 800K disk, click the Two-Sided button, as shown in Illustration 3.7. The Mac initializes and verifies the disk; you can then use it like a brand new blank disk. Click Cancel in either little dialog box to get out of it without erasing the stuff on your disk. For more details, see page 31.

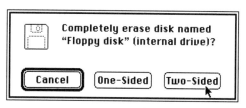

Illustration 3.7: Erase disk dialog box

RESTART: Checks the Mac to make sure your work is saved, then shuts it down and starts it up again. Unless you put a startup floppy disk in the drive at the beep or chord sound, it will start on the hard drive.

SHUT DOWN: Checks the Mac to make sure your work has been saved, then closes any open applications and shuts all software

Special
Clean Up Desktop
Empty Trash
Eject Disk ⌘E
Erase Disk...
Restart
Shut Down

Illustration 3.8:
Special menu

down, then displays a dialog box on a black screen saying that it is now safe to turn the Mac off. You can also click the Restart button in this box to restart the Mac.

On portable and PowerBook Macs you may have two additional commands: **Sleep,** which turns off the system, but leaves active applications and documents in memory, so you come back to them immediately when you click any key or the trackball button, and, on some older models, **Rest,** which just turns off the screen and hard drive. For more information on these battery-saving commands, see page 72.

BALLOON HELP MENU

Menu for getting information about the Desktop's parts and Finder shortcuts. This menu is only available on Macs running System 7 and later.

ABOUT BALLOON HELP: Displays a message box that tells how to use the balloons to see information about the desktop. Click OK to close the message box.

SHOW BALLOONS: Turns on the little messages in balloons, so you can point at things on the desktop and see explanations of them.

HIDE BALLOONS: Replaces Show Balloons when the balloons are turned on. Turns off the balloons, so you don't go crazy trying to get your work done with all those balloons popping up.

FINDER SHORTCUTS: Displays a window with a bunch of very useful keyboard shortcuts for actions you take on the desktop, like actions having to do with icons, windows, and outline (list) views. Also tells the keyboard combinations that do crucial things like rebuilding the desktop, taking a snapshot of what

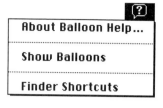

Illustration 3.9:
Balloon Help menu

is showing on the screen, or turning off all extensions at start-up time. Click the close box to get out of the window.

APPLICATION MENU

Menu for choosing the Finder and any other applications you have opened, so you can switch back and forth between them. This menu isn't like any of the others. For one thing, it's only available if your Mac is running Multifinder, or System 7 or later. For another thing, its title and its content change, depending on whether you are using the Finder or an application you have opened. If you are in the Finder, the menu icon will be a little Mac. If you are in an application, the application's icon appears in that space. To open the menu, pull it down from whatever icon is at the far right end of your menu bar. In addition to listing open applications,

Illustration 3.10:
Application menu

the menu lets you hide any windows of the Finder or the applications that you aren't using at the moment. Although it will probably take you some time to get use to the peculiar form and function of the Application menu, you will learn to love it if you have to do lots of switching back and forth from applications to the Finder, or switching between two applications, like between a word processor and a spreadsheet or a graphics application.

HIDE FINDER: Hides all the open Finder windows and switches you into the last application you were using. Choose Finder from the application to get back to the Finder.

HIDE OTHERS: Hides all the open windows of the applications other than the Finder. Makes it easier to see the Trash can, in most cases. Choose any application from the application menu to see its windows again.

SHOW ALL: Puts all of the open windows of the Finder and other applications back in view on the desktop.

FINDER: Puts you in the Finder; displays the desktop.

APPLICATIONS: Switches you to any of the listed applications; the list depends on which applications you have opened.

CHAPTER 4

25 Tips to Keep You and Your Mac Smiling

This chapter lists 25 of the most useful tips for keeping you and your Mac happy. The first 10 are for you, directly; things you can do or keep in mind at all times when using the Mac. The second ten tips are things you can do to keep the Mac working at maximum efficiency and minimum crash rate. The last 5 tips are especially for PowerBook users. Some of the tips, especially the ones toward the end of each section, may not make sense to you until you have used the Mac for a while. Don't let that bother you; those tips are rarely important to new users, anyway. But as you build up experience on your Mac and also build up lots of files and folders over time, you should come back and look through these tips again, so you can benefit from the ones that require more experience.

10 Tips to Keep You Smiling

These tips are for you; use them to become a more powerful, satisfied Mac user.

1. FIRST *SELECT* WHAT YOU WANT TO *AFFECT*

This means that you have to highlight an item before you can choose a command that does things to it. For example, to change the title of a folder, you have to select the old title first, then you can type the new title. This rule works in thousands of situations; if you ever feel stuck when you're trying to do something, try selecting the item in question with the pointer before you take any other action. It works, it works!

2. SAVE OFTEN AND MAKE BACKUP COPIES

When you are working on any document, from creating the master pages for a 500-page book to sketching a flower in Kid Pix or editing a memo in TeachText, choose **Save** from the File menu or press ⌘-S every ten minutes or so; that way, you won't lose your latest work if there is a power surge or the program crashes. At the end of each day, or when you finish a day-size chunk of work on something, back up the document; for details on backing up, see page 102.

3. WHEN YOU MAKE A MISTAKE, TRY UNDO IMMEDIATELY

You can often undo actions you have taken on the Mac, from misspelling a word to deleting your last two hour's worth of work. To undo your boo-boo, choose **Undo** from the Edit menu, or press ⌘-Z. Not all actions can be undone in this way; if the **Undo** command is grayed out in the Edit menu, or if it says "Can't Undo" in gray letters, your last action is irrevocable. Also, if you make a mistake and then go on to another action, you usually cannot go back and undo the mistake. For example, if you select a word, then press backspace, then type a new one, you can't undo the deletion and get the original word back; if you choose **Undo,** the new word just disappears. On the other hand, if you delete a bunch of text by selecting it and choosing **Cut** from the Edit menu, then type some new text, you CAN still get that cut text back. Just select the new text and choose **Paste** (⌘-V) from the Edit menu.

4. QUIT APPLICATIONS YOU AREN'T USING

When you finish using an application, you can leave it open and go open a second as long as you are using System 7 or the Multifinder, which was the part of the older versions of the Mac system software that let you use several applications at once. But unless your Mac has lots of RAM (like at least 4Mb), you should close each application after finishing with it. If you don't, you will use up more and more of the Mac's memory as you open new applications, until the Mac either gives you a "Not Enough Memory" message, or crashes. The Mac may wipe out your latest work as it freezes up or bombs. See page 134 for details on these problems.

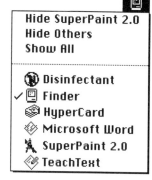

Illustration 4.1:
Application menu with lots of applications open

If you have enough RAM to open two applications, you can do so and switch quickly from a document in one application to a document in the other; this makes it easy to cut and paste between the two. For example, you can draw a picture in a graphics application and paste part of it into a text document. Or you can write and edit some text in a word processor, then copy it to the Clipboard and paste it into a graphics image. Whee! Just don't open and use more applications than your Mac's RAM can handle. For more information on memory issues, see page 90.

5. EMPTY THE TRASH REGULARLY

If you are ever looking at the desktop and notice that the trash can is full (it bulges when there's stuff in it), choose **Empty Trash** from the Special menu. A warning message box appears, telling you how much stuff you are about to permanently remove. Click OK to go ahead and empty the trash. The can loses its bulge.

If you are NOT SURE you want to throw away the stuff in the trash, open the trash window and look through the items in there. I use the **by Date** view of the items, so I can see when they were last modified; that sometimes jogs my memory of what the thing actually is and if it is the latest version I have.

If you are VERY SURE you want to delete the stuff in the trash every time you empty it, then you can turn off the warning message box; to do this, select the Trash can, then choose **Get Info** from the File menu. When the Info window opens, click the checkbox in the lower left corner, to turn off the "Warn before emptying" feature. But be careful; it's easy to empty forgotten documents that turn out to be valuable.

If you empty some trash that you need after all, you may be able to recover it, especially if you make your recovery effort soon after dumping. See page 139 for details.

6. LOCK SOFTWARE DISKS; PROTECT ALL DISKS
FROM MAGNETS, DUST, AND HEAT

When you buy a new application to install on your Mac, Open the little square door in the corner so the disk is locked; this protects it from anybody altering the application software, and it protects the disk from viruses, too.

You can also lock floppy disks that have stuff on them that you don't plan to use for a long time. For example, if you finish work on a big project, you can lock all the disks containing the backups of the final versions.

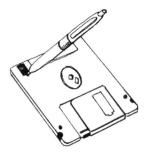

Keep all disks, both applications and documents, away from things that can wreck them. Don't leave floppies in the hot sun or by a stove, don't get magnets near them (this includes the

Illustration 4.2: Locking a disk with pen tip

magnets inside TV tubes and inside your Mac's monitor), don't open the little metal door and touch the floppy disk inside with your fingers, don't get dust on your disks, and don't spill wet stuff on floppies or drop them into water.

7. USE ELLIPSE COMMANDS IF YOU ARE A NEW USER

If you are just learning to use the Mac or a new application and aren't sure what a command does, don't hesitate to choose it if it has three dots after it. Commands with dots after them are ellipse commands; each one calls up a dialog box that lets you make some decisions before putting the command into effect; you need to click an OK button in the dialog box to set the command in motion. You can also click a Cancel button if you decide the command is not what you had in mind after all.

For example, if you are working on a document and want to print it out, but you're not sure whether you should use the **Print...** or **Print Preview...** command, you can just go ahead and try the **Print...** command, and then click OK in the dialog box to start the printing job.

If you choose a command with no dots after it, you have to just put up with what the Mac does, unless you can choose **Undo** from the Edit menu immediately after choosing the command. For example, if you edit something you have done, and you aren't sure whether you should save the edit or not, you can get in trouble by choosing the **Save** command from the File menu. This command saves the document with the editing changes you made and usually deletes the previous, unedited version of the document. **Save** cannot be undone, either. A better choice would be the **Save As...** command, which lets you save the edited version of your document with a new name; the previous, unedited version of the document is retained with its original name, too. You can also choose to Cancel the saving process in the Save As dialog box.

When you become more familiar with the commands, you will, of course, use the ones without ellipses as much as or more than the ellipse commands; only choose ellipse commands when you are unfamiliar with the menu you are looking at.

8. MAKE SURE YOU HAVE ENOUGH RAM

This means make sure your Mac has enough memory in it to do the work you want to do. And then some. It is a fact of computer life that new, more powerful versions of applications and system software ALWAYS need more and more memory than the older, weaker versions. This means that you will never regret adding RAM (Random Access Memory) to your Mac, especially if it came with only 1Mb or 2Mb. You can probably get by with 4Mb of RAM; this much allows you to open one or two powerful applications under System 7 and create normal-size documents. But if you are into color, big spreadsheets, page layout, or any other memory-intensive type of work, you may need much, much more than 4Mb of RAM. For more details on memory management, see page 90.

9. KEEP YOUR SYSTEM FOLDER SMALL AND TIDY

This means limit the stuff in your System Folder to things you really need. If you are a new user and you aren't messing with the System Folder, you won't have to worry about this problem. Installing system extensions and control panels is what can make your System Folder get fat and messy. So, you power users, don't add every gimmick extension and shareware control panel you can get your hands on. And if you use an extension or control panel for a while, then decide you no longer need it, remove it from the System Folder. The same advice goes for Fonts and Sounds, too. Don't just keep adding more and more. The System Folder is the workbench for all that the Mac does. If you clutter it up, the Mac will have trouble working quickly and efficiently. For details on saving memory by slimming down your system software, see page 112.

10. KEEP YOUR FOLDER HIERARCHY CLEAR AND SIMPLE

Name each folder with a title that describes the contents, and nest folders in a way that makes sense. Don't have more than ten folders at any level of the hierarchy and don't make the hierarchy any more than four levels deep, if you can help it. On the other hand, don't be afraid to put lots of files in one folder if that makes sense. For details and examples, see page 78.

10 Tips to Keep Your Mac Smiling

These tips are for the good of your Mac. Use them to improve the computer's performance and keep it from crashing.

11. PLUG EVERYTHING IN CAREFULLY AND KEEP IT PLUGGED IN

Firmly plug in the power cord for the Mac and, if they are separate units, the monitor and/or external hard drive. Plug the cables for your mouse and keyboard in carefully, too, then plug in any peripheral devices you have, such as a printer, a network connection, a scanner, or special monitor. If you plug in SCSI devices, make sure they are terminated properly. DO NOT unplug anything while the Mac is on. For details, see page 7.

12. DON'T MOVE THE MAC WHILE IT IS ON

If your Mac has a hard disk inside it, you should not move the Mac at all while it's turned on. If the Mac is reading from or writing to the hard disk and gets jostled roughly, the "heads" (they work somewhat like the playing and recording heads on a tape cassette player) can bounce on the disk and either self-destruct or ruin the disk. Most new hard disk drives (especially those in PowerBooks) have built-in protection against these "head crashes," but don't take any chances. If your Mac is connected to an external hard drive, don't move the drive while it is on; it has the same vulnerability as a hard drive that's inside the Mac.

The most common mistake that causes disk damage is sliding the Mac or hard drive over the surface of a desk. If the device starts to shake or bounce as it slides, that can be enough to crash the heads during a read or write.

13. REBUILD THE DESKTOP OFTEN

This means to let the Mac do some housecleaning. All you have to do is hold down the ⌘ and Option keys as you start up or restart your Mac. The system software then removes outdated records of changes to files and folders; these records are stored in the hidden "desktop file." Removing the outdated records slims down the desktop file, so the Finder can work better and more quickly.

Rebuild your desktop about once every week or two if you shuffle lots of files and folders around. Also rebuild it if you notice that it takes an unusually long time to switch from an application back to the Finder or to complete the part of the startup sequence going from the Welcome screen to seeing the desktop.

There is one drawback to rebuilding the desktop; comments in the Get Info boxes for all files on the hard disk are lost. For this reason, I never put comments in the little box at the bottom of any file's Get Info window. For more details, see page 106.

14. DEFRAGMENT YOUR HARD DISK
ONCE A MONTH OR SO

This means to rearrange all the files stored on your hard disk, so the Mac can get at them more easily. As you open, save, close, and delete files on the hard disk, they get broken up into fragments to fill the empty spots that appear on the disk. Soon there are so many fragments in so many places that it takes the Mac a long time to find an entire file, put it together, and open it for you.

Use a defragmenting or optimizing utility, such as Speed Disk (part of a great collection of helpful tools called the Norton Utilities for the Macintosh). If the utility has an option that lets you check the disk for fragmentation, check it every month; if there is significant fragmentation, go through the optimization or defragmentation process. On large hard disks, or with slow

Macs like the old Plus, it can take quite a while, like an hour or more, to defragment a badly fragmented hard disk, so you should do it during your lunch break or something. For more information, see page 106.

15. KEEP ONLY *ONE* COPY OF THE SYSTEM SOFTWARE ON YOUR MAC

The system software is what keeps the Mac running. The Finder and the System file are two critical parts of the system software. The Mac must have one copy of the Finder and the System file in the System Folder of the disk it is running off, but no more than one copy of each. If you install extra copies by mistake, or if you leave a floppy with copies of the system software in your Mac, there can be big trouble. The computer can get confused and lock up, crash, or lose your precious documents.

The only times you need a second copy of the system software are when your hard disk crashes or when you are using a special disk tool, such as a virus-protection application or a defragmenter. If you crash, you have to insert a startup disk with a copy of the system software on it, so the Mac can pick itself up and get going again. See page 136 for details on this situation. If you are using a virus-protection tool to disinfect your hard disk, or a defragmenting tool to defragment it, you have to run the Mac with system software on the same floppy disk with the disk tool, so that you can run your Mac from the floppy while the tool is working on the hard disk; this is somewhat like using a loaner car from the garage while they work on your car.

To make sure you have only one copy of the System file and the Finder on your hard disk, just choose **Find...** from the File menu and look for the two files. After finding the first copy, choose **Find Again** from the File menu. You may have to wade through a number of files with titles that contain the word "System," but just make sure there are not two files simply called "System" in the System Folder. If you have a handy utility like Fast Find (of the Norton Utilities) you can locate all of the files with the word "System" in them and see them displayed all at once.

If you locate more than one copy of either the System file or the Finder, remove whichever is the older version; if the older version is the one in the System Folder, reinstall all of your system software, using the latest version available. It's best to get help from an expert Mac user or a complete manual like *The Macintosh Bible* to make sure you install the system software properly.

16. DON'T RESTART, SHUT DOWN, OR TURN OFF THE MAC WHILE IT'S READING FROM OR WRITING TO A DISK

This is just common sense. If the Mac is trying to save something you created from its memory to a disk, you don't want to turn it off and lose the stuff. If the Mac is reading something, you don't want to turn it off and lose the data, either. ALWAYS choose **Shut Down** from the Special menu in the Finder before you reach for the power switch. If you always use **Shut Down,** the Mac will complete all saving before it tells you it's safe to turn it off. If your Mac crashes and you have to turn it off without shutting down, rebuild the desktop when you start up again, as described in Tip #13 of this chapter.

17. DO THINGS ONE AT A TIME

This means don't choose menu commands or do keyboard commands while the pointer is a little watch or a spinning beach ball icon. The Mac's CPU can only do one thing at a time. Usually it can put a second command from you on hold while it is still working on your first one, but sometimes it gets confused or stuck, or the application crashes. So if you choose a command that takes the Mac a few seconds to complete, wait until the pointer or insertion point reappears to take your next action.

18. IF YOU HAVE AN EXTERNAL HARD DRIVE, MAKE SURE IT IS ON WHENEVER THE MAC IS ON

This simply means that if you have a hard drive that is separate from the Mac, such as a SCSI drive, you must turn it on before you turn the Mac on, and you must wait to turn it off until you have turned the Mac off.

A few rare older hard drives do not park their heads (the little thingies that read from and write to the hard disk) automatically when you turn the power off; for these exceptional cases, obtain a software utility that parks the heads and shuts down the Mac; then turn off the Mac and turn off the external hard drive last, as usual. You can get such utilities as SCSI Stop from someone in your local user group or an on-line information service.

19. IF YOU HAVE SEVERAL SCSI DEVICES, MAKE SURE THEY HAVE DIFFERENT ID NUMBERS

This is only important if you have more than one SCSI drive, scanner, or other SCSI device. You must find out how to set the SCSI ID number on each device (there is usually a little dial with numbers on the back of the device) and set them so that they are all different and all between 1 and 6. It is best to give your main hard drive the number 6, especially if it is your start-up drive (the one with the system software on it). Give low-priority devices, such as scanners, low numbers such as 1 or 2.

20. KEEP THE MAC COOL

That means don't use it in the hot sun, especially if it is a Plus. Mac Pluses are wonderfully quiet without fans but they are vulnerable to heat. If you have a Mac or hard drive with a fan and vents, make sure the vents are never blocked off by books (including this one), pillows, paper, or anything else. If you can see filters inside the vents for your fan-cooled hard drive, use a vacuum to clean the dust off the filters once a year or so. Or take the hard drive to a qualified technician for a yearly clean-out. Some people even add fans to old Macs to make sure they stay cool.

5 Tips to Keep Your PowerBook Smiling

The 20 tips listed above are for all users of almost all Macs. But just for you hot-shots who are using PowerBooks, here is a short collection of tips that apply to your mini-Macs alone.

21. PLUG YOUR POWERBOOK IN WHENEVER POSSIBLE

Don't run the PowerBook off its batteries unless there is no way to plug it in. It won't run longer than a couple of hours in most situations, and if you are really crunching numbers or doing other CPU and disk-intensive work, the batteries can run down in much less than two hours.

22. SAVE BATTERY LIFE BY TURNING BACKLIGHTING OFF AND USING SLEEP MODE

To turn backlighting off, just use the brightness control that's below the screen. If you have good natural lighting or strong artificial lighting, you don't need the backlighting. Sit next to the window on the plane. If you have to use backlighting, at least set the screen to dim automatically when idle; use the PowerBook Display control panel to do this. To shorten the time your Mac sits idle before it goes to sleep, first make sure your system soft-

ware is updated to 7.1 (if it is, there will be a big black dot next to the "7.0" in the About This Macintosh window when you open it from the menu). Then open the PowerBook control panel and move the slider toward the right end; the setting that's farthest to the right puts the system to sleep after 1 minute of idle time, and puts the hard drive to sleep after half a minute. The next setting to the left is for 4 and 2 minutes of idle time before system and hard disk sleep mode, and the next setting is for 8 and 4 minutes of idle time. Of course, if you know you are going to be leaving the Mac idle for a few minutes, or even 1 minute, you can always save the battery by going to the finder and choosing **Sleep** from the Special menu. You can save some more battery life by turning off AppleTalk if you don't need it and turning off any communication software if you aren't using a modem. Finally, if you have lots of RAM, set up a RAM disk and run your PowerBook from it rather than the hard disk. For details on this trick, see Cary Lu's "PowerBook Notes" in the February 1993 issue of *Macworld* magazine. One final battery-saving trick: if you have any of the PowerBooks that run at 33 Megaherz (145, 160, 170, or 180) and you are using version 7.1 of the system software, you can go to the PowerBook control panel and put the Mac at Reduced speed. The battery savings are great, but you may find things like number-crunching pretty slow.

23. SHUT DOWN YOUR POWERBOOK BEFORE YOU CONNECT OR DISCONNECT PERIPHERALS

It's tempting to plug things into a PowerBook when it is in sleep mode, and some people plug and unplug certain peripherals (such as a mouse) even when the PowerBook is wide awake, but I say, don't risk it. You can short things out if a plug goes into a port wrong, and the short can blow the teensy little fuse on the main board of the computer; this can lead to a very expensive repair.

24. DON'T STARE AT YOUR POWERBOOK SCREEN FOR LONG PERIODS

Even the best gray-scale screens on the PowerBook are not as easy on your eyes as standard black-and-white monitors for compact and modular desktop Macs. If you have to work for long hours on your computer, either connect it to an external monitor or upgrade to a Macintosh Duo system that allows you to dock your PowerBook in a desktop unit with a large, clear CRT monitor.

25. IF YOUR 140 OR 170 POWERBOOK WON'T WRITE TO A DISK, TURN DOWN THE BRIGHTNESS

I know that sounds weird, but it is true. Some 140 and 170 PowerBooks have a nasty bug that blocks copying or saving to floppy disks. When you turn down the screen brightness control, the disk drive starts whirring. If it works, don't argue with success. Be thankful and thrive.

CHAPTER **5**

Organizing Your Stuff
On the Mac

This chapter tells you how to put things in good order on your Mac and how to maintain that order as your files and folders build up over time. You'll see how to put all your documents and applications in folders, and how to organize the folders into a hierarchy that makes it easy to find and store things. You'll also see how to organize everything in your System Folder, like your extensions, control panels, and items in your menu; these are things you can use every day, and you'll be more liable to use them if you can find them easily. Finally, you can learn how to organize the Mac's storage and memory so you get the most out of it.

Organizing Your Folder Hierarchy for File Storage

In the "File and Folder Basics" section of Chapter 2 you learned that folders are containers for files and folders, and files are all the individual items on the Mac. The documents you create and edit when you work in applications are files, but so are the applications themselves and all the little utilities and even the pieces of the system software that make the Mac work. In short, everything you see an icon for is a file unless it is a folder.

The trick is to organize all those files into folders that make sense, so when you need to find some document or application, you can locate it quickly by looking in the logical folder. If you organize files by putting related ones in a folder that has a good name for the group of files, and if you organize related folders into other folders that have good names for the groups of folders inside them, you wind up with a hierarchy, a sort of pyramid of folders and files. If it is a good hierarchy, it will be easy to find things in.

Does making a simple hierarchy sound complicated? The best way to understand it all is to begin creating a hierarchy for your own applications and documents.

To make this basic hierarchy, use the instructions in "Making folders and files" and "Organizing your hierarchy" below. If you are new to the Mac, start out by following the example just as it reads, even if you can't see what the logic of the organization is. Have faith. Later, you can adapt it if it doesn't meet your needs or suit your style. If you are an old hand at the Mac and already have a hierarchy of folders that works well for you, just use the example as a guideline for putting your hierarchy into a nice, neat order. I'm not trying to say that the hierarchy I outline here is the only way to do things; it's just a commonly-used set-up, and it gives you a framework to build on.

Two rules of thumb are good to follow as you build your hierarchy:

• Try to keep less than ten files or folders in any folder; that's how many you can see in a typical file list in an Open or Save dialog box

• Try to limit any folder hierarchy to less than five levels, so you don't have to hunt up and down through lots of levels to find things

These two rules not only make life easier for you as you work your way around your hierarchy, they also make it easier for your Mac and the Finder to deal with all the files and folders.

MAKING FOLDERS AND FILES

To make a folder appear in the active window in the Finder, all you have to do is choose **New Folder** from the File menu or press ⌘-N. The folder shows up with the name "untitled folder." You can type in a name for the folder immediately.

For example, to start building your own folder hierarchy, open your hard disk window, then choose **New Folder** from the File menu. Type the word "Applications." You now have a folder for storing all your applications (if you already have an Applications folder, skip this step). To make a folder for letters and memos, press ⌘-N again, then type "Correspondence." You should already have a System Folder in your hard disk window (by the way, don't move or open or mess with the stuff in that System Folder until you have done some reading about it or are following clear, specific instructions; you can cripple your Mac very easily by tampering with the System Folder).

There are two ways you make files on your Mac. You install application files onto your hard disk, and you make document files by using the applications.

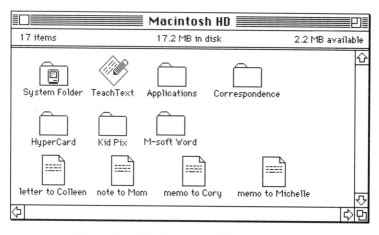

**Illustration 5.1: A bunch of files and folders
in the hard disk window**

To get some application files, buy and install applications that you need, following the manufacturers' instructions for installation. See "Application Basics" in Chapter 2 for more information. You probably already have TeachText and HyperCard somewhere on your hard disk, especially if you have a new Mac. TeachText is an application file. HyperCard is usually inside a folder called HyperCard. If you install other quality applications, anything from Kid Pix to Microsoft Word, each application will usually be in a folder of its own. You can see the actual application file if you open the folder's window.

For example, if you double-click the HyperCard folder, you see the application file and any other files that HyperCard uses. Close any application's folder window when you're done looking in it, so you have just your hard disk window showing.

Once you have some applications, you can make documents by opening the applications, doing some work, then saving the work, as explained in "Application Basics" in Chapter 2. For example, you can open TeachText, write a letter to Colleen, a note to Mom, and memos to Cory and Michelle (or whoever you want to write things to). If you save each of those documents when you are done writing, you wind up with four, as in Illustration 5.1.

If you open an application that's inside a folder, like Microsoft Word, notice that the documents you save show up in the Microsoft Word folder, not the hard disk window like the TeachText documents. To make things look like Illustration 5.1, you have to use the tricks for saving in a different folder that are explained in "Saving your work" on page 36, or just drag any documents in an application's folder to the hard disk window. This may take some moving and resizing of windows. See the "Windows Basics" section of Chapter 2 if you need help.

ORGANIZING YOUR HIERARCHY

OK, you now have a bunch of icons in your hard disk window showing folders, applications files, and documents. Here's how to make a nifty hierarchy out of them.

First drag the icons for all the letters, notes, and memos into the Correspondence folder. Then drag all of the applications (such as TeachText) and application folders (such as the HyperCard folder) to the Applications folder. Don't move the System Folder. It has to stay right where it is, in your hard disk window, so the Mac knows where to find it at all times; the Mac depends on the system software that's inside that System Folder to do everything, remember.

Notice how the setup forms a sort of pyramid, with the hard disk at the top. If you open the hard disk window, you will only see the System Folder, the Applications folder, and the Correspondence folder.

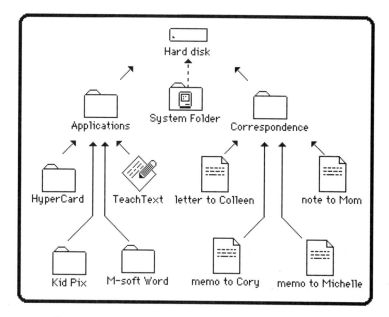

Illustration 5.2: A simple hierarchy of files and folders

USING A LIST VIEW TO SEE MORE AT ONCE

If you are wondering what is in all those folders scattered among your new files in the hard disk window, you can use a list or "outline" view to take peeks into folders. Just choose **by Kind** or **by Name** from the View menu. Illustration 5.3 shows my simple hierarchy in a list view by kind. The files and folders are all listed in the window, and every folder has a little triangle next to it, which you can click to either show what's in the folder (when the triangle points down) or hide the list of the folder's contents (when the triangle points to the right). If this list view of your files and folders is easier for you to deal with than the icons, just leave the window in a list view and go on with the procedure of building your folder hierarchy. For more information on using list views, see pages 54-56.

Aah, such a nice, simple hierarchy. Nothing confusing, nothing extraneous. But life never stands still. Confusion and extraneous files always sneak in, like jackals out of the wilderness. You make more files, and more folders to hold those files, and pretty soon, the old hard disk window starts looking messy.

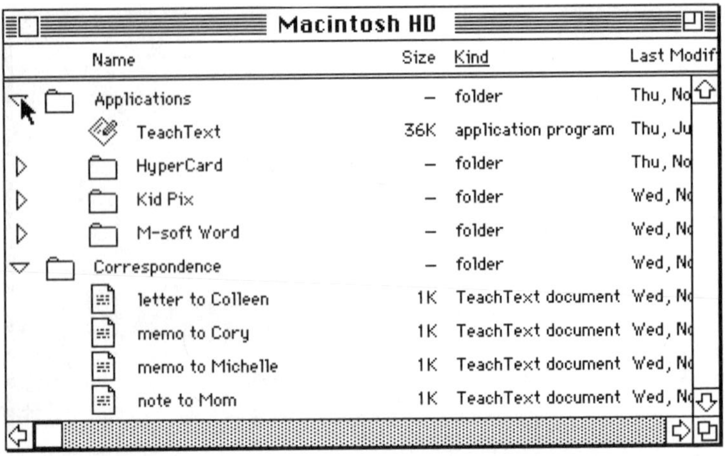

Illustration 5.3: A list view (by Kind) of a simple hierarchy

Not to worry. All you have to do to take care of this confusion and mess is add to your simple hierarchy as you need more layers. For example, if you write lots of memos and letters, you can make a Memos folder and a Letters folder. Or, if you are working on a project, you can make a folder for it and give it a good name. In my case, for writing this book, I have a folder called Back Pocket; in it I have a document for the text of each chapter and a folder for all the artwork in each chapter. That keeps all the artwork and the text files from cluttering up my hard disk window. See how it works? You can really put a lot of files in just a few folders if you organize and name them clearly.

There is no rule that says you have to make a hierarchy just like the one shown and described here. You may have different needs or a different style of organizing things. Some people like to organize all their documents by date in monthly folders, for example. Some people like to keep all documents created by an application in the same folder with the application. Others like to have all documents in alphabetically ordered folders, one for each letter of the alphabet. Build the hierarchy that's best for you.

Don't lock yourself into an organization, either. If there is one application or one document that you use much more than all others, it makes sense to have an alias for that item out on the desktop, in the hard disk window, or in the menu, so you can get at it quickly. An alias is like a copy of the icon for an item. It lets you open the item from someplace other than where you keep the item tucked away in your folder hierarchy. No sense in digging all the way down into all those folders when you can just keep an alias of a much-used document or application out in the open where you can double-click it immediately. For more on using aliases, see page 29.

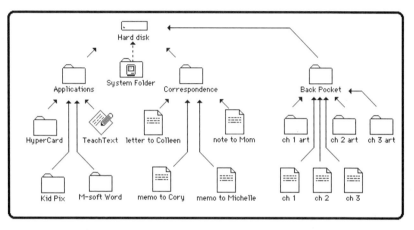

Illustration 5.4: Hierarchy with a project folder

Finally, when you have lots of files and folders, it's good to have a folder in your hard disk window set aside for items that need to be put away in other folders, and another folder for miscellaneous-small-stuff. That way, if you can't figure out where to put something, you can tuck it in the "needs-to-be-put-away" folder, then take time to figure out where it goes later. And you can put all those little files of vague origin and use in the miscellaneous-small-stuff folder. Sometimes I build up a whole hierarchy of folders in a subfolder inside miscellaneous-small-stuff, and when it gets big enough and important enough, I just move the subfolder out into the hard disk window.

So let your hierarchy grow and adapt it to your needs as they grow and change. Accept a little messiness in the hierarchical order. As Carol McQuilling (a great thinker and dancer who has passed away) used to say, "Lots of life, lots of mess!" Just maintain a good hierarchical structure to contain the mess.

Control Panels, DAs, and Extensions

These are things you find in your System Folder. Control panels are generally things you use to adjust how particular aspects of the Mac look or work. DAs are desk accessories; little programs that do special jobs above and beyond what your applications do. The difference between DAs and applications is becoming more and more of a gray line as time goes on. Extensions are things that extend the power or functions of the Mac system software. Some are included with your system software, but many more are available for adding hot-rod power to your Mac.

If you ever have any trouble with a control panel, DA, or extension, you can take it out of your System Folder and be rid of it. It makes sense to remove any of these things that you never use; they use up hard disk space and memory, too. For more information, see the "Reducing memory use" section at the end of Chapter 6.

USING CONTROL PANELS TO CUSTOMIZE THINGS

There are a whole bunch of control panels you can use to change everything from what the desktop background looks like to what time the Mac's clock reads, to what font is used for list views.

I like most control panel settings just as they are, the way the nice people at Apple set them. There are good reasons that Apple picked the standard or default settings they did. I recommend you also leave all control panels set at their Apple defaults until you get used to the Mac a bit. But as you learn your way around the desktop and start to make use of the Mac's many powers, there are a few adjustments you will certainly want to make, such as setting the Mac's clock. Most of the rest of the stuff you can figure out on your own and play with on your own time, as far as I'm concerned.

SETTING THE CLOCK AND DATE

To set the clock you use the General Controls panel. First choose **Control Panels** from the menu. Open the General Controls window by double-clicking its icon. When the window opens, select the AM/PM setting, then the hours, minutes, and seconds

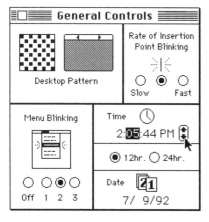

Illustration 5.5:
Adjusting the time

in the Time panel. Use the up and down arrows to adjust each setting. You can set the date, then you can change to a 24-hour reading if you are used to military time. As for fiddling with the rate of in-sertion point blinking, the number of times a menu choice blinks when you select it, and the pattern of the desktop background, you're on your own. I like 'em all as they are (well, I have to admit that when I work on a color monitor, I change the desktop background to royal blue). You can also adjust the time and date whenever you need to by opening the alarm clock DA, as explained in "Using DAs" later in this section.

ADJUSTING THE MOUSE RATES

This has nothing to do with how much the mouse charges you. The mouse works for free. But you can adjust how fast the pointer moves, or *tracks,* when you move the mouse, and how quick you can double-click with the mouse button.

To make these settings, first choose **Control Panels** from the menu, then open the Mouse control panel window. When the window opens, click in the buttons for the mouse tracking speed and double-click the speed you want. I like the fastest for both, but I've been mousing around for a long time. You should probably start with the second-fastest settings, then move up to the fastest after a little practice.

ADJUSTING BRIGHTNESS

This is for making the screen brighter or darker. All you have to do is choose **Control Panels** from the menu, then double-click the Brightness icon. A slide bar appears, as shown in Illustration 8.1. Drag the slider to the right to make the screen brighter and to the left to make the screen darker. I have found that the best setting is just a bit brighter than the level of light on the wall behind the Mac. If there is a strong contrast between the brightness of the screen and the brightness of what is behind the Mac, your eyes will get strained and headaches will follow.

ADJUSTING COLOR

This is to turn color on, if your Mac and monitor can show color, and to adjust the colors so they suit you. First choose **Control Panels** from the menu and double-click the Monitors icon. Click the Colors button in the Monitors window, then choose the number of colors you want to see in the list box. In most cases, 256 colors works best, assuming your Mac and monitor are up to the job of processing and displaying all those shades. Restart your Mac to see the colors. If you want to change the colors of the highlights or window trim you see in Finder windows (application windows often have their own color scheme!), open the Color control panel and choose colors you like from the pop-up menus in the color window. If you don't like any of the colors, you can choose Other from either pop-up menu and play with a color wheel to specify the color of your dreams. If you want to change the color of your whole desktop, open the General Controls panel and fool with the Desktop Pattern settings. To get a wider range of colors, just double-click any of the colors in the color bar below the Desktop Pattern, then click on the color you want in the color wheel. Click OK, then drag the pointer around in the magnified view of the desktop pattern (the one on the left) to fill in the color, and finally, click in the unmagnified view of the desktop (to the right of the magnified view) to make your new color take effect.

ADJUSTING VIEWS

This is to change what you see in windows in the Finder. You can't make most of these adjustments in versions of the system software prior to System 7. Choose **Control Panels** from the menu, then double-click the Views icon. The Views window opens, with a section for the font for all views and sections with settings for icon and list views.

• To change the font or font size of the text you see in Finder windows, use the pop-up menus at the top of the window.

Geneva 9 point is the default; it allows the maximum number of items to be listed in a window. If you have really crowded windows, get Skinny Font from your user group or an information service; it is similar to Geneva, but more compressed horizontally.

• To change how icons line up in icon views, click the buttons for straight or staggered grid; to keep all icons lined up all the time, put a check in the "Always snap to grid" checkbox.

• To change the size of the icons that appear in list views, click the buttons under the small, medium, or large icon. I like the middle size; lots of them fit in a window, but they are big enough to show some hints of what kind of icons they are.

• To show the sizes of folders as well as files in list views, put a check in the Calculate folder sizes checkbox. I only do this when I'm scanning my folders to see which ones are overstuffed and need to have files deleted out of them or copied to floppies.

• To show the disk info header in list view windows as well as in icon view windows, put a check in that checkbox. I don't do it unless I'm really short of disk space and deleting stuff to make some room.

• To show the size, kind, label, date, version, and comments for files and folders in list views, put checks in the appropriate checkboxes. I only show the size, kind, and date to keep list windows from getting too wide.

Try out the different settings, especially the list view ones, and figure out which combination works best for you.

USING DAS

DAs (desk accessories) are really just mini-applications. You choose them from the menu, which means you can use them any time, even while using another application. Since you can now switch between applications and the Finder anyway, via the Application menu, the convenience of DAs in the menu is no longer so important, but it can still be nice for quick work. One neat thing about DAs; when you close the window for one, the whole DA quits for you. This keeps the Application menu short and memory free. Some of the most commonly used desk accessories are the old Apple standards: the alarm clock, the calculator, the Chooser, Key Caps, the Note Pad, and the Scrapbook. There are improved and expanded versions of these Apple-supplied DAs, but some of them aren't cheap. Look for them at the larger dealers, or check your local user group or the on-line information services.

ALARM CLOCK

Opens a small box that tells you the time. Click the little flag at the right end of the box to open up a larger box, with options for setting the time, setting the date, and setting the alarm to go off. When the alarm goes off, you hear a beep (or whatever sound you use for a beep) and the alarm clock icon flashes alternately with the ⌘ menu icon. To stop the flashing icon, open

**Illustration 5.6:
Alarm clock**

the alarm clock box, expand it, and select the alarm clock, then click the switch to the left of the alarm setting. The switch goes down and the alarm shuts off. You can get fancy improvements on the standard alarm clock, such as ones like SuperClock that display the time near the right end of the menu bar (if there is room) and others that ring musical chimes on the hour. Not for me. There are also DAs that remind you of repeating events or things you have to do over a period of time. These are very handy for us forgetful professor types.

CALCULATOR

Opens a little window that looks and acts like a pocket calculator. You can enter equations by clicking the buttons in the calculator window, by pressing the number keys at the top of your keyboard, or by using the numeric keypad at the right end of most keyboards. You can copy the numbers that appear in the calculator display box and paste them into documents, or you can cut or copy numbers from documents and paste them into the calculator's display box. You can get improved versions of the calculator that do all kinds of intensive number-crunching, but that kind of stuff works best on high-powered Macs with math coprocessor chips. Over my head.

CHOOSER

One DA you can't live without. Lets you choose the printer you want to send your documents to for printing, and if you are on a network, lets you choose the zone and server you want to connect to. For details, see pages 117 and 118.

KEY CAPS

Lets you see a picture of a keyboard with the characters of the current font displayed, so you can see what character will be produced with each key, including the Shift and Option keys. To see other fonts, you choose them from the Key Caps menu. It's OK, but slow and clumsy. I like the improved version called KeyFinder, by Norton. It just shows you a big chart of all the possible characters in the current font, and when you select one, a little box on the right shows you what keys to hit to enter the character. Like, in Helvetica, if you select the in the table, you see that you have to press Option-Shift-K to enter that character. Another handy key utility is PopChar; it lets you pull down a menu from the corner of your screen and click on any character you want in the current font. It's shareware, so get it through your user group or from an information service.

NOTE PAD

Lets you keep eight short text notes. A very simple little thing, but it can be useful for storing notes about things you are using for a particular project; when you are done with the project, you can erase the notes or replace them with others. The current notes do not go away when you shut down the Mac, however. To see them, just choose **Note Pad** from the menu, then click in the turned up page corner down at the bottom of the note pad to leaf through the pages of notes.

SCRAPBOOK

Lets you store text, graphics, or other items so you can copy them whenever you need them in an application. You place things in the scrapbook by cutting or copying them from a document into the clipboard, then pasting them into the scrapbook. They stay there until you select and cut them. They don't go away when you shut down your Mac. You get things out of the scrapbook by copying them into the clipboard, then pasting them into the document of the application in which you are working. For details on the clipboard, see page 53.

The last thing you paste into the scrapbook is always shown first. You can move an item to the front of the scrapbook by scrolling through until you see it, then choosing Cut from the edit menu, then scrolling to the front of the scrapbook (the left end of the bar) and pasting the item there. This is a pretty primitive way of organizing things, but it works OK if you have only five to ten items that you need to get at often. If you do lots of cutting and pasting and need to have a large, well-organized scrapbook, consider getting an improved version of the DA, such as SmartScrap or ClickPaste.

ADDING CUSTOMIZING EXTENSIONS
AND CONTROL PANELS

There are many, many files that you can add to your Mac's System Folder to increase the power of the system software and add to the general quality of your Mac's look and feel. In the old days they were often called INITS (because they take effect as the Mac is initializing its RAM at startup). There are screen savers that do all kinds of weird things like show fireworks or fractal splatters on your screen when you leave the Mac idle for a while. There are utilities that do everything from organizing your menu and defragmenting your hard disk to digging through the emptied trash, and there are extensions that guard against destructive viruses and save files from accidental deletion. Some extensions and control panels add handy choices to your ⌘ menu, so you can use the added features any time you want.

If you install a bunch of DAs and custom utilities and add them all to your ⌘ menu, it can get so long it'll be hard to use. But fear not, there are custom control panels that help solve this problem, too. My favorite is HAM, which stands for Hierarchical Apple Menu. It lets you put things inside folders in your ⌘ menu and organize the items in the menu however you want. My ⌘ menu only has about ten items in it, but some are folders that let me get directly to things like Control Panels, recently opened documents and applications, and often-used utilities such as the Norton ones. Oooh, it's so nice! You can get some of the same ⌘ menu enhancements from a shareware program called MenuChoice, but in my experience, it is a bit clunky and not as powerful as HAM.

Choose extensions carefully; they may seem like wonderful improvements, but some can cause more trouble than they fix. Talk to other users and read what the magazine reviews have to say about them before buying and installing them on your Mac. Make sure any extension you buy is compatible with your Mac, your version of the system software, and the other applications and extensions you have installed.

One way to make sure you get a bunch of extensions that work well is to buy a complete kit, such as the Norton Utilities for Macintosh, MacTools, or the Now Utilities. I'm a fan of Norton. Most of the Norton utilities are very simple to install and use, and thay don't bog down the system software or other applications. They have saved me from many a mishap, quickly and reliably.

If you want to install several extensions that are not part of a group, add them one at a time. Drag the icon for each extension to the closed System Folder icon in your hard disk window. Before installing another extension, shut down and restart the Mac. If you have problems, take off the last extension you added. If you really have problems running the Mac after adding extensions, restart it and hold down the Shift key. This turns off all extensions. When the desktop appears, open the System Folder and Extensions folder and take all of those pesky things out. Then put a few in at a time and restart the Mac, to see which one or ones caused the crash or hang-up. Weed out the problem extensions and use the others. If you want to use lots of extensions, but don't need to use all of them at once, and you want to minimize conflicts, get an extension manager such as INITPicker or Ask of the MockPackage utilities.

Managing Storage and Memory

When you buy a Mac, you have to decide how much memory and storage to get. Do you want a Classic 2/20 or 4/40? How about a PowerBook 180; do you want it with 4/80 or 8/120? The 180 is the model number, we know that, but what do those pairs of numbers mean? In each pair, the first number tells how many megabytes of RAM the Mac has, and the second number tells how many megabytes of storage there are on the hard disk. It's hard to even keep all the numbers and their meanings straight when you are shopping for your first computer, but you find out, as you use your Mac, that these numbers are not only very important, but impossible to ignore. You keep RUNNING OUT of either memory or storage, or both.

No matter what combination of memory and storage you buy, you often wind up with less than you need later on. When there is a shortage of memory or storage, the Mac can have problems. It can suddenly stop working, or *crash*, for instance. So, to avoid memory and storage problems, you need to understand what these two things are and how to manage them wisely.

What is the difference between memory and storage? Memory is in the Mac's chips, and storage is on disks. The Mac can get at its memory and use the things in it very quickly, but everything the computer has in memory is completely lost and forgotten the minute you turn the Mac off. Storage is more permanent; it usually consists of either floppy or hard disks. Floppy disks are in little plastic cases with metal doors; you know what they look like because you have a bunch around, I'm sure. You have either 800K floppy disks with one little square hole in a corner, or 1.4Mb hard disks, with two little square holes in two of the corners. A hard drive looks much like a miniature record player, but the disk is much thicker than a record. It takes the Mac a bit of time to get at (access) the stuff in storage on disks, but data is not lost when you turn the Mac off. Unless something unusual happens to a disk, the stuff the Mac puts on it stays there, safe and sound, until you need it.

Memory is the part of the Mac that can hold info and pieces of applications while the Mac's brain, or CPU (Central Processing Unit), works on them. The bulk of the Mac's memory, the part that you have to deal with, is temporary; the Mac can change and move things in and out of it at any time. That's why it's called Random Access Memory, or RAM. When you start an application, the Mac reads the key parts of it off the disk where it is stored and puts it in RAM for quick use. When you open a document, the Mac reads it off disk storage and puts as much of it as possible in RAM, too. Then the CPU can get at the application and the document quickly and do the work you want to do as fast as possible.

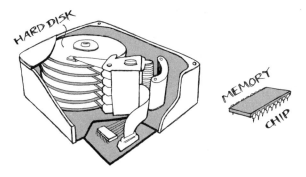

Illustration 5.7: Storage disks and memory chip

RAM is like a kitchen counter; storage is like kitchen cabinets. To fix dinner you get your utensils and ingredients out of the cabinets, then you work with all of them on the counter. When you're done, you clear everything off the counter and put the utensils and leftovers away. The system software is like a multi-use cutting board; you can dice on it, slice on it, mix and knead and mash on it, but it doesn't change much; it just has to be there, under all your work and taking up counter space, at all times. If you left the cutting board and all the other utensils and food on the counter day after day, it would get so cluttered and messy you couldn't work there. Similarly, if you kept everything in RAM, it would fill up and become useless. Every time you turn off your Mac, the RAM is cleared completely, so you can start with a fresh workspace when you turn it on again. The only thing that appears on the counter automatically is that cutting board—the system software. It controls all the comings and goings, so it has to be there as a base for all your other work tools and ingredients.

To keep your RAM from getting too cluttered as you work, you need to check how much of it you are using with your applications and documents, and you have to know how to clear the decks when things are getting too crowded. To make the best use of your storage, you need to learn how to set up and organize hard disks and floppy disks. The subsections below cover these topics.

There are a few other descriptive details about memory and storage that should be included here for completeness. The following paragraphs cover them very briefly. These aren't things that most of you will ever need to be concerned with.

Some of the Mac's memory is built in at the factory, and the info in it is unchangeable; this is called Read Only Memory, or ROM. When you do any simple action on the Mac, like pull down a menu, the Mac reads how to do it in its ROM. But you never have to do anything to the ROM to make it work. If the basic functions on your Mac stop working, like you can't pull down menus anymore, first try rebuilding the desktop and reinstalling the system software. If those things don't help, take the Mac to a qualified repair technician.

There are several kinds of storage other than hard and floppy disks that you may come across at some time. There is tape drive storage, which is commonly used for backing up large amounts of information on large computer systems. For personal Mac use this doesn't make sense because it takes much longer to access info on a tape than on a disk. There are removable hard disks that you can use like high-capacity floppies, switching them in and out of the hard drive. These are great for storing large amounts of data for different projects separately. There is also CD ROM, which is good for storing large amounts of reference information, such as a computer encyclopedia or collections of complex color graphics and sounds.

CHECKING YOUR RAM USE

This means seeing how much memory your applications and the system software are using and how much RAM is still free. To monitor RAM use, you need to be in the Finder (choose Finder in the Application menu), and when the desktop appears, choose **About This Macintosh** from the menu. A window opens, showing you data about how your Mac is using its memory supply.

If you are using a version of the system software prior to System 7, you have to quit your application or click the MultiFinder icon to get to the Finder, then choose **About the Finder** to see how your Mac's RAM is being used. Alas, you can't make the adjustments to allocations that System 7 users can.

The following list explains what each of the elements in the window tells or shows you (see Illustration 5.8).

• Total Memory: Tells you how many kilobytes of RAM you have installed in your Mac. In the sample Mac, 4,096K, or 4Mb. In the kitchen metaphor, this means the size of your counter.

• Largest Unused Block: Tells you how many kilobytes of RAM are still not being held for use by the system software and applications. In the sample Mac, 594K. In kitchen terms, this means how much space is still free on your counter.

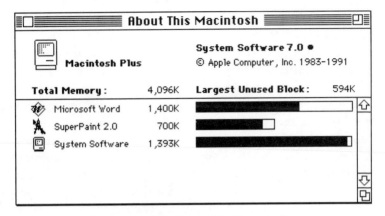

Illustration 5.8: About this Mac window

• Amounts per application: Tells how many kilobytes of RAM are reserved for each application in use and how many are reserved for the system software. In the sample Mac, 1,400K is reserved for Word, 700K for SuperPaint, and 1,393 is set aside for the system software at the moment.

• Dark and light bars: Show you how much use is being made of the RAM allotted to each application and the system software; the dark part of each bar is the part of the allotted RAM being used, and the light part is the part still unused. In the sample Mac, Word is using about 66% of its allotted RAM, SuperPaint is using about 80% of its RAM, and the system software is using about 90% of its RAM.

If the largest unused block of RAM is tiny, like under 20K, and you are getting "Not enough Memory" messages, you need to close at least one application. If you HAVE to keep all the applications open, you need to decrease the amount of memory allotted to each application, add RAM to your Mac (the best solution), or see Last Ditch Memory Saving below.

If any of the application bars is almost all dark with no light, you need to increase the amount of RAM allotted to it. Don't worry about the system software bar being almost all black, though; the system software is so clever it can adjust its own RAM allotment any time it needs to.

If you see "Not enough Finder memory" messages or crash often while doing things between applications and the Finder (such as saving, opening, or copying big files), it often means you have an extension that is not playing fair or trying to rip off RAM from the system software (for more info on extensions, see the preceding section of this chapter). Turn off all your extensions by holding down the Shift key as you restart your Mac; if this solves your memory problem, you know you have a naughty extension (if the problem persists, see page 138). Take them all out of the System Folder, then put them back in a few at a time, narrowing down the list of possible culprits until you find the RAM-grabber. See the manufacturer or programmer who wrote the extension and get a version that doesn't steal RAM.

If the makers of an extension tell you that all you have to do is increase your system heap (that's jargon for the portion of RAM that's set aside for the system software), tell them politely that as you understand it, this is a temporary cure to the problem, and you want a more permanent fix, namely, a version of the software that plays fair and deals wisely with the system software and RAM allotments. Increasing the system heap simply means increasing the system software's RAM allotment. If the extension is stealing or messing things up in its dealings with the system software's memory manager, increasing the system heap just gives it more to steal or more freedom to be messy; you may have more memory shortages and crashes at some time in the future.

ADJUSTING HOW RAM IS ALLOCATED

To increase or decrease the amount of memory set aside for an application, first you have to quit it. Then, in the Finder in System 7 (sorry, but this stuff doesn't work on the older versions of the system software), find and select the icon for the application and choose **Get Info** from the File menu. In the Info window for the application, select the number for the current size in the lower right corner. Increase the number by 10% or 20% if you need more and have enough unused RAM to do it. For example, if you have 1,024K set aside for Word and you keep running out of memory, increase the current size to 1,400K or more. If you are short of unused RAM and need to reduce the current size, you can do so, but try to keep it at least as big as the suggested size; if you go below that, you run a risk of trouble with large documents and memory-intensive jobs such as spreadsheet calculating and text formatting or spell-checking. After entering the new current size, close the Info window. You can then open the application with its new amount of allotted RAM.

ADDING TO THE DISK (RAM) CACHE

If you notice that repeated actions (such as saving, opening list view windows, updating the page number of a text document, or redrawing

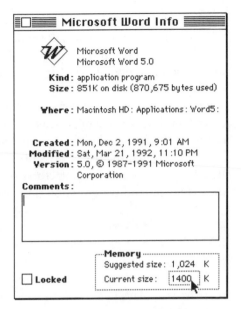

Illustration 5.9: Info window for Word, raising current size to 1400K

a graphic) are slow, you can set aside some RAM to speed up those actions. Choose **Control Panels** from the menu, then open the Memory control panel. At the top of the Memory window there is a Cache Size box that tells you how many kilobytes of RAM are set aside for repeated actions. Click the Use Defaults button at the bottom of the window to see how much RAM the system software guesses you should set aside; it depends on what model of Mac you have and how much RAM there is overall. If you usually have at least a few hundred kilobytes of RAM in your largest unused block of memory in the About This Macintosh window, then you can surely set aside more RAM for those slow repeating actions. For example, if your default disk cache size is 16K, you can increase it to 128K or 192K, and you'll notice a great improvement in performance. If your default is 128K, you can increase it to 256K or more; the improvement may not be so obvious, but it will be clear when you repeat actions that take a long time.

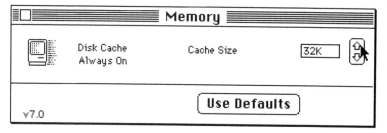

Illustration 5.10: Memory window, increasing disk cache size

LAST DITCH MEMORY SAVING

If you are really short of RAM (you can't open all the applications you need to use) you can lower the size of the disk cache, even setting it below the default size, but this may slow your Mac down to a snail's pace when you do repeated actions, so you should only do it as a last resort.

There may be buttons for turning on virtual memory and 32-bit addressing in your Memory window. I chose not to show them in Illustration 5.10. I don't think either of them makes sense for most normal use of a standard Mac by a novice or intermediate Mac user. In some power-user, memory-intensive, special-application situations they make sense, but for us normal folks, it's best to leave both virtual memory and 32-bit addressing off.

ADDING RAM

This means adding memory chips to your Mac. They come in the form of Single In-Line Memory Modules (SIMMs), and depending on which Mac you have, you can upgrade to 4Mb, 8Mb, 10Mb, or more. To run two standard applications and the Finder under System 7, you need at least 4Mb. Most of us need from 4Mb to 8Mb to do our work. You may need more if you are using color or 3D graphic applications, or if you work with complex page layout documents, big spreadsheets, or multi-media stuff. If you need lots and lots of RAM, you can get special 16Mb SIMMs that stack up the chips for maximum use; just make sure these special SIMMs are designed for use with your particular model of Mac.

You can install SIMMs in your Mac yourself if you make sure you never get any static electricity on them and don't bump or short out any of the Mac's vital parts. Installing SIMMs is easy to do on modular Macs such as the LC or Mac II models. It is a good deal trickier to open, upgrade, and reclose a compact Mac such as a Plus or Classic. Notebooks and Portable Macs can only be upgraded by a shop. For an excellent article on adding RAM, see the May 1992 issue of *MacWorld* magazine. Thanks to Shelly Brisbin for her superb work.

If you are leery of adding those static-sensitive SIMMs yourself, you can have a qualified technician do it; an upgrade usually only costs about $25 to $50, added to the price of the SIMMs. It's worth that much to be sure that the memory is right for your model and that its working correctly.

SETTING UP YOUR HARD DRIVE STORAGE

Before you can use a hard drive, it has to be set up properly; if it is an internal hard drive it has probably already been set up by the factory or the previous owner. If you are adding an external SCSI hard drive to your Mac, see page 7 for details on things like plugging in the correct cable, setting the SCSI ID number, and termination. They are critical details for proper operation of an external SCSI hard drive. Once you have set up your hard drive, all you have to do to use it is open the window for it and start dragging things into it, putting them in appropriate folders. For more information on creating and using folders wisely, see the "Folders and Files" section later in this chapter.

CHECKING HOW MUCH STORAGE SPACE YOU HAVE

This means seeing how many megabytes or kilobytes of free space there is on your hard disk. (If you are using only floppy disks, you can use the info in this section as a guide, but you should REALLY get a hard drive; they are so cheap now, and they make life so much easier.) To see how much of the storage space on your hard disk you have used up and how much is still available, all you have to do is open the window for your hard disk and look at the information bar that is just below the title bar. If you don't see the information bar, you're probably looking at a list view of the window; just choose **by Icon** or **by Small Icon** from the View menu and the information bar appears.

The information bar tells you how many items are on the disk, how many megabytes of space they occupy in the disk, and how much space is still available. This information is good, but limited. For example, you can have a couple of megabytes of space left on a 40Mb hard disk and still be flirting with disaster; some hard disks can crash and destroy all of your data if they are working with less than 10% of the space free, and if they are badly fragmented. Disks get fragmented over time; the files are broken up into pieces and scattered around to fill in blank spots on the disk, and eventually they can get so scattered it's hard for the Mac to put them together when you open them.

Illustration 5.11: Info bar

To get the full picture of how full your hard disk is and if you need to defragment it, use a utility, such as Speed Disk in the Norton Utilities collection. See page 106 for details.

COPYING FROM ONE FLOPPY DISK TO ANOTHER

This is one detail of disk storage that takes some getting used to. All you need to do, really, is drag one floppy's icon over the other floppy's icon. That's easy if you have two floppy drives, but it can be baffling if you have only one floppy drive. There's a way to do it with a minimum of switching disks. First, insert the DESTINATION floppy disk in the disk drive; this is the blank disk you want to copy stuff onto. If its window opens, close the window, but leave the floppy icon selected. Chose **Eject Disk** from the Special menu, or if you have system software prior to System 7, choose **Eject** from the File menu. When the destination disk spits out, it leaves a ghost icon behind on the desktop (note: if you drag a floppy's icon to the trash or choose **Put Away** from the file menu, the disk spits out and leaves no ghost behind).

Once you see the destination disk's ghost icon, insert the SOURCE floppy disk with all the stuff you want to copy. When the icon for it appears on the desktop, drag the icon to the ghost icon for the destination disk. Click OK in the dialog box that asks if you want to replace everything on the blank disk with the stuff on the source disk. Switch disks when the Mac asks you to; you should only have to switch the disks two or three times.

You can use this same procedure for copying just a few files or folders from one floppy to another, too. Just open the source disk's window, then drag the items you want to copy to the ghost icon of the target disk. It usually only takes one disk-switch to get the job done.

There are several utilities that can make the job of copying from one floppy to another even easier. I like Floppier, which comes with the Norton Utilities, but there are others such as DiskCopy and Copy II Mac that work just as well.

There are some limitations on copying from one kind of disk to another. These limitations are due to the fact that old Macs have drives that can only read 800K floppies, and new Macs have SuperDrives that can handle both 800K and 1.4Mb floppies. The best rules of thumb are:

• If you have a later model Mac with a SuperDrive and ONLY work with that Mac, you can use 1.4Mb disks and copy all info from one to another.

Illustration 5.12: Dragging source floppy icon to destination floppy

• If you have an older Mac without a SuperDrive, you have to use 800K disks.

• If you have a SuperDrive but work with other Mac users who have 800K drives and need to exchange information on floppy disks, then you should ALL use 800K floppies.

You can get into peculiar jams trying to copy between 1.4Mb floppies and 800K ones. For example, if you format a 1.4Mb floppy as an 800K one on an old Mac, then put data on the disk and take it to a SuperDrive Mac, the SuperDrive Mac will try to reinitialize the disk and erase all your precious files. Agh!

CHAPTER 6

Housekeeping

This chapter tells you how to take care of a few important Macintosh maintenance needs. These are things you just *have* to do every once in awhile, like washing the dishes and putting books back on the shelves. You need to do some of the tasks quite often; others can wait for a week or even a month, depending on how much you use the Mac and how much you change things around on it.

Saving and Backing Up

These are the things you do to make sure you don't lose any of your valuable documents, the things you have created and edited with applications. The basic techniques of saving your work are covered in the "Application Basics" section of Chapter 2.

SAVING OFTEN

When you save your work by choosing **Save** from the File menu or pressing ⌘-S, the Mac takes all of the new work you have done, or the changes you have made to an existing piece of work, and writes it to the hard disk or floppy disk you specify. Once the document has been saved on a disk, your work is safe from accidents or mistakes; you can quit the application, the software can crash, or the electricity can suddenly go off, and the saved document will still be there, safe and sound, when you get things working again.

So save often. It is so quick and easy, you have no excuse to overlook it. Many people try to save every 15 minutes. I'm more erratic. If I'm doing something that is really labor-intensive, I may save twice every 15 minutes. On the other hand, if I am composing a tough chapter and the work is going slowly, like at the rate of a page an hour, I may not save for a half hour or so. But I always try to save before I leave one application to go work in another, or before I get up from the Mac and go do anything in another room. It's so*oo* easy to forget that the Mac is on (especially if it is a nice quiet one), and then you can come back an hour later and find that the power has had a little surge or momentary cutoff, and all your work is GONE. Agh. By the way, it's also a good idea to plug your Mac into a surge suppressor, or even an uninterrupterible power supply if you live in a place where the power tends to go out often.

BACKING UP

Even if you save your work on a hard disk, you can still lose it. Hard disks can crash. It doesn't happen often, but sooner or later, almost every hard disk goes blotto or "hoses" (destroys) some files. There are things you can do to avoid these catastrophes, like setting up your hard disk carefully (see page 98) and defragmenting (see the section on defragmenting later in this chapter), but it is still good to back up your work as a kind of insurance.

You can do backups in lots of different ways. You can just copy documents to floppies. You can use a backup utility to copy and/or compress all your data onto floppy disks. Or you can back up with a utility to a spare hard disk. Finally, if you have tons of data to back up and want a cumbersome but cheap backup scheme, you can get a tape drive and periodically back up everything on your hard disk. The following paragraphs cover the first three types of backups. Tape backups are really for network administrators or big-time power users, so I'll leave them to the specialists.

1. MAKING SIMPLE BACKUP COPIES: If you don't work on huge documents, and don't create lots and lots of them every day, you can do a very simple form of backup; just copy the most important documents from your hard disk to a floppy disk. If you change the documents, you can replace the old backup copies with the modified copies. It's easy to list the contents of any folder by Date, and just drag all the documents at the top of the list (down to the first one with a "Last Modified" date older than the date of your most recent backup) to your backup floppy's icon. The Mac asks you if you want to replace the older documents with the same names. Click OK, and the modified documents will replace the old ones. The only problem with this method is that you can't go back to an old, unmodified document if you decide the newer, modified one is a mistake. The worst thing that can happen is that you replace a nice, well-finished document with one that has the same name but (by some fluke or accident) no data in it. To safeguard against this kind of nightmare, I always check the size of documents as well as their date. I figure it's pretty safe to replace an old document with a newer one that is close to the same size or bigger.

2. USING BACKUP UTILITIES TO BACK UP TO FLOPPIES: If you produce lots of documents in lots of different folders and want to make sure you lose nothing, you can get a utility that will take care of all your backup work. Some of the more simple utilities, such as Redux and AutoBack, just make copies of your data; others, such as Norton Backup, FastBack, and Retrospect, can compress files as they save them, so you don't use up so much disk space. You can set up most utilities so that they either back up everything (this is known as an archival backup) or back up only the things that have changed. Most utilities also let you exclude things from the backup, like hidden system files that change as you work. If you back up only your changed files, you can save the old backups or copy over them. The high-powered backup utilities can do either incremental or differential backups. But they are often complex and hard to figure out; unless you do lots of backups, you tend to forget how to use all the powerful features between backups. If you get frustrated, you might avoid doing backups altogether. I have fairly simple backup needs, so I find Norton Backup to be adequate and very easy to use. If I were doing the backups for a whole network of Mac users, I'd probably use a utility like FastBack or Retrospect.

3. BACKING UP TO AN OLD HARD DISK: One backup option that is simple and cheap is to get a used (but reliable) hard drive and use it for backing up your documents only. If you lose some applications in a crash of your primary hard disk, you can always reinstall the applications from the original program floppy disks you bought. Saving your daily changes of documents in one or two folders is pretty quick and easy. The major risk in this method is forgetting to back up new documents in new folders. Keep your documents well organized, in only a few folders, and you probably won't forget to back anything up. If you tend to forget about backing up, you can use this backup-hard-drive method, but get a utility like AutoBack to do the copying for you. AutoBack makes a backup copy every time you

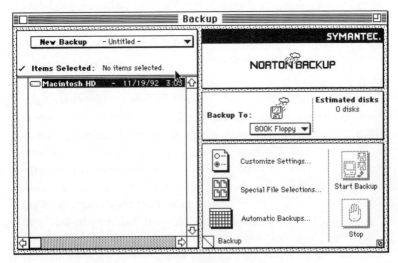

Illustration 6.1: Backing up with Norton Backup

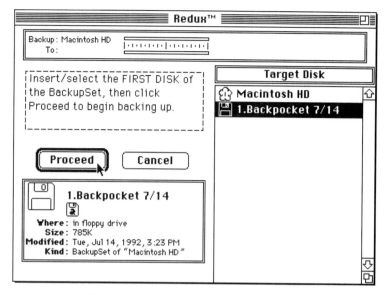

Illustration 6.2: Backing up with Redux

save a document. This is an especially good option for small networks, where people share documents, and everybody thinks the other guy is doing the backing up.

Rebuilding Your Desktop

Sounds kind of formidable, doesn't it? I mean, you imagine tearing the legs off the thing, or at least cutting the trash can apart and welding it back together. How can this be a good thing for you or your Mac?

Not to worry. All you really do is clean out the desktop file; an invisible file that records all the creating, moving, copying, deleting, and renaming of files and folders that go on as you work in the Finder. This file isn't ever visible to you; the Mac just keeps all that obscure data to itself. But it gets bigger and bigger over time. Old and obsolete information stays in it as well as the info that's current. Since the Finder has to look through it every time you switch to the Finder from an application or start up the Mac, it can drag down the Mac's performance. And the desktop file can get damaged if you have a crash. So do yourself and your system software a favor and rebuild your desktop once a month or so. If you do lots of moving, copying, deleting, and renaming of files and folders, rebuild once a week or even more often. It doesn't hurt to do it often.

TO REBUILD THE DESKTOP, just hold down the ⌘ and Option keys as you start up or restart the Mac. A dialog box appears, asking if you really want to do it. Click OK. A message box shows you the progress of the rebuild.

The one drawback to rebuilding the desktop is that it erases all your comments in the Info boxes for applications, documents, and folders. These are called Finder comments. If you want to recover them, you can use Norton Utilities. You have to have the FileSaver utility turned on. Then, after rebuilding your desktop, you just open the Norton Utilities and choose Restore Finder Comments from the Options menu. There are also shareware and freeware utilities, such as Maurice Volaski's CommentKeeper, that will save Finder comments for you. Check with your local user's group or information service to find such a utility.

Defragmenting Your Hard Disk

As you use your hard disk, copying and saving files onto it, deleting files off it, and updating files as you work on them, you fill up the disk. As it gets close to full, the files start getting broken into little pieces and scattered all over it. This scattering of the files is known as fragmentation. Some people think this has something to do with compressing files, but it is quite different. Compressing files is reducing them to the minimum size, so you can fit more on a disk; you use a special utility, like StuffIt, to do the compression. Fragmenting is spreading the pieces of a file (either a compressed or a full-sized one) around on the disk to make use of all the little blank spaces that appear as the disk is used. The Mac does this fragmenting as you use it, without ever letting you know that it is happening.

Fragmentation happens because the disk's driver software (the program that places files on the disk) writes the files in any empty space it can find. Space on the disk is divided up into small units. As the disk gets close to full, pieces of files are placed in all the little leftover units of space between other files. As you go on adding and deleting new and old files, the little empty units of space become more and more scattered, so your new and updated files get divided up into more and more little fragments and placed all over the disk. Then when the Finder comes looking for a file, it has to do a lot of hunting around and collecting fragments before it can show you the file and let you go to work. This is hard on the Finder. It is also hard on the hard disk if it gets so bad that the disk has to thrash around looking for those little pieces all the time.

If it takes your Mac a lot of extra time and disk-spinning to open an edited file, or if you see a message box saying "The application is busy or missing" when you try to open an application you *know* is right there in front of you and not busy at all, then your hard disk is probably fragmented.

To defragment a hard disk, you need an optimizing and defragmenting utility. It should be a high-quality, easy-to-use utility, so there is no chance you will lose any documents or applications on the hard disk as the utility takes all the files off it and puts them back in a new and optimal order. I like Norton's Speed Disk. It is wonderfully easy to use, clear, and reliable. It not only puts all the file fragments back together, it organizes all your documents, applications, and system software in a way that speeds up the performance of the disk and your Mac. This organizing process is called optimizing, and it's a great thing to do for the health of your hard disk and the performance of your Mac. The rest of the information in this chapter applies directly to Speed Disk, but you can use it as a guideline for any brand of defragmentation or optimization utility.

Before you defragment any hard disk, make sure that you have backed up everything on it, especially the documents you have created. Applications can be reinstalled from the floppies

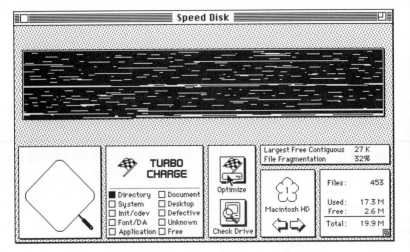

Illustration 6.3: Speed Disk ready to defragment

you bought, but if a document gets lost or damaged during defragmenting, it's gone for good.

TO DEFRAGMENT (or optimize, as they say) with the Norton Speed Disk utility, first start up your Mac using the Norton Application Disk 1; turn on the Mac and immediately insert the Norton Application Disk 1. When the Welcome to Macintosh window goes away, the Speed Disk window opens up automatically. It shows a picture of the layers of data on the current disk, which is the Norton Application Disk 1. To see how your hard disk looks, click either of the big arrows under the icon for Application Disk 1.

When your hard disk's icon appears, look at the picture of the file fragments at the top of the window and see if there are lots of little white blips of space scattered all over and no big blocks of white space (as shown in Illustration 6.3). Click the Check Drive icon to get a report of just how much fragmentation there is and whether you need to defragment. I defragment if there is even moderate fragmentation. If you want a more detailed report, choose **Go To Expert** from the Options menu. Then Speed Disk tells you the largest chunk of free contiguous space it could find on your hard disk and the percentage of the files that are fragmented. As a rule of thumb, I defragment when I have less than a megabyte of free contiguous space, or when more than 10% of the files are fragmented.

In some cases you may need to defragment with even more free contiguous space or less file fragmentation. For example, if you have a large file that you use often, such as a huge database or graphics file, and you hear the hard disk thrashing all the time as you work, then you should defragment, even if the Check Drive report says only 5% of your files are fragmented. Similarly, if you have virtual memory turned on, and it is trying to use several megabytes of space on your hard drive to back up the RAM (UGH, the idea revolts me, but it is necessary at times), you should defragment and even delete some stuff off your hard drive to create that free contiguous space, or the hard drive is going do a lot of spinning every time you start any memory-intensive task.

To start the defragmentation of your hard disk, all you have to do is click the Optimize button, as shown in Illustration 6.3, but before you do, you may want to make some performance-improving adjustments to Speed Disk. Optimization can take a half hour or more on a slow Mac, even if you're only defragmenting a moderately fragmented 20Mb hard drive.

To speed up the defragmenting process in Speed Disk, there are several things you can do. First choose **Show Pencil** from the Options menu if there is a check next to it. This unchecks the option, so the little pencil icon goes away and the display of progress on your hard disk updates faster. This means the defragmenting goes faster. For even less show and more go, choose **Go To Expert** from the Options menu, then choose TurboCharge from the newly extended Options menu. This cuts the reports and screen updates to a minimum and turns off the color display, so you can't watch the defragmenting as closely, but the job gets done more quickly. Another good trick is to increase the amount of memory allotted to Speed Disk. First quit Speed Disk. Then, in the Finder, select the Speed Disk icon on the Application 1 disk. Next choose **Get Info** from the File menu. In the Info box, raise the current memory size to at least twice the suggested size; the extra RAM can go to memorizing larger amounts of the files as they are defragmented.

Reducing Storage and Memory Use

If you have a relatively small hard disk and a relatively small amount of RAM in your Mac, you will often be confronted with shortages of either storage or memory. What does it mean to have a relatively small hard disk or a relatively small amount of RAM? All it really means is that the storage and/or the memory you have is less than what you need. You might have a 500Mb hard drive and 8Mb of RAM and still run short of both storage space and memory if you are using lots of applications at once and cranking out huge color graphics documents in TIFF format. On the other hand, you might have a Classic with a 20Mb hard disk and 2Mb of RAM and still get along OK, as long as you just create simple 20K-50K documents using a single application that isn't a memory hog. So don't think you have to have as much storage and memory as somebody else; just watch for warning signs like "Not enough memory" and "Not enough room on disk" message boxes.

SAVING STORAGE SPACE—CHECKING FOR
BIG FOLDERS ON YOUR HARD DRIVE

This means looking for stuff you can take off the hard drive to free up some empty space. First choose **Control Panels** from the menu, then open the Views control panel. When the Views window opens, click the checkbox for Calculate folder sizes so

that there is an X in it. Close the window, then open your hard disk window if it isn't already open. Choose **by Size** from the View menu; it will take a moment or so for your Mac to calculate all the sizes of the folders showing in your hard disk window. You may be quite surprised at which folders are using up the most disk space.

Click the triangle next to the icon for any folder that is suspiciously large in size. Look inside for large files and subfolders that you don't ever need to use, or rarely need to use. The first places I always look for stuff I won't need are my Applications folder and the folders that contain documents from projects that I am finished working on. For some weird reason I am often hesitant to move documents from last year's projects off the hard disk; it's as if I expect a publisher to call me up and tell me that they've lost all the copies of my book. If you have limited storage space, you can't be squeamish that way. Make good backups of those precious documents, then delete them from the hard disk to make room for the future.

SAVING STORAGE SPACE— COPYING, BACKING UP, OR DELETING

These are the three ways to get stuff off your hard disk so you have more free space to work with. Use the method that suits your needs, either for easy access to the files or for large savings of disk space.

• If you have outdated documents you want to keep handy, and lots of floppies and some spare time, just copy your old documents onto floppy disks, name them and mark them clearly, and store the floppies somewhere safe and close at hand. Then drag the copies that are still on the hard disk to the trash, empty the trash, and check your hard disk window's information bar to see how much more space you have on the drive.

• If you have lots of big documents that you want to save, but aren't going to need to get at real often, the efficient thing to do is back them up on floppies or another hard disk. If you want to save disk space, check out the backup or archiving utilities that can compress your documents as they back them up, such as Norton Backup, FastBack, Retrospect, or StuffIt Deluxe. Some of these utilities are easier to use than others. If you aren't a hot-shot with backup techniques, you should find a utility that is easy for you to use, so you don't lose things in the shuffle or waste a lot of time getting at a file that is on a backup disk. Also keep in mind that some compression utilities are safer than others; StuffIt has a long reputation for reliability, for instance; other compression utilities tend to leave things out now and then. For more details on backing up, see page 102.

• If you have some files that you are sure you will never need again, or that you are sure you have backup copies for already, you can just drag them to the trash. For example, if you have an application on your hard disk that you never use, and you still have the original program disks that the application came on, first check out the old program disks to make sure they are still OK, then you can drag the application file and all its accessory files out of your hard disk window and into the trash.

SAVING MEMORY

This is about using your memory as efficiently as possible. If you only have 2Mb of RAM and you want to run System 7, you're going to have to use every trick listed here, and maybe more. If you can possibly afford to do it, buy some SIMMs before you start trying drastic measures to save on memory use. 4Mb memory upgrades are pretty cheap, and the difference between 2Mb and 4Mb is dramatic, especially for System 7 users. But no matter how much RAM you have, you may see "Not enough memory" messages now and then, so use the following solutions (listed in the order that you should try them) to get out of any memory shortage jam. To check on how memory is being used up, choose **About This Macintosh** from the ⌘ menu in the Finder; see page 93 for details.

• If you don't need to keep all the currently open applications on tap, quit at least one of them. Just choose Quit from the File menu and save any changes to documents if you see a reminder message.

• If you are sure you have more memory than the Mac thinks (check the largest unused block size, as explained on page 93), you may have fragmented the memory by opening and closing several applications in succession. To defragment your fragmented memory, quit all applications, restart the Mac, and open the applications up again. To prevent fragmented memory, always start the most-used, most-memory-greedy application first, and the little seldom-used ones later.

• If you are not using any networking software, remove the Network extension and the File Sharing extension from the Extensions folder in your System Folder. If you don't even need to print over an AppleTalk connection (if you have a printer that just connects directly to your printer port, instead of a laser printer with AppleTalk connections, say), you can turn off AppleTalk in the Chooser. See Illustration 7.2 for details. When you have removed the network extensions and/or have turned off AppleTalk, you need to restart your Mac to free up the memory they used.

• If you use lots of PostScript outline fonts, you can put them in a separate place and clean all the TrueType and most of the bit-mapped fonts out of your System file. PostScript is the page description language used by most laser printers, and the PostScript fonts have wide acceptance in the desktop publishing world. Putting all your PostScript fonts in their own folder and cutting out the others is a big project requiring some advanced Mac skills, but if you are a desktop publisher, it is worth the trouble. See a comprehensive manual, like *The Macintosh Bible,* or a good book on using PostScript fonts.

• If you have cut or copied a huge object to the clipboard (such as a big color graphic or a long text document), get it out of there by copying a small object (such as a single letter or a dot).

Copy it twice, so the big object gets flushed out of the clipboard and out of the "Undo buffer," too.

• If you are using network software, or if you may need to now and then, get the latest version of the System 7 tune-up and install it on your Mac; it helps keep network software from hogging all your RAM.

• If you have a lot of extensions, DAs, and control panels that you never use, take them out of the Extensions, Apple Menu Items, and Control Panels folders in your System Folder and put them in another folder. I keep such things in "Disabled extensions," "Disabled DAs," and "Disabled control panels" folders, so I can find them easily. If the extensions, DAs, or control panels are defective (like, funky freeware instead of well-tested shareware or commercial stuff) and cause trouble by conflicting with other things, I say you should just trash them. The fewer extensions and control panels around, the better the Mac works.

If all else fails, you can reduce your disk cache (RAM cache). To do this, choose **Control Panels** from the menu, then open the Memory control panel. In the Memory window, reduce the size of the disk cache. This will slow down the Mac for some operations, however, and make the CPU work overtime.

Finally, if you still don't have enough RAM to open a large application, you can reduce the amount of memory allocated to it. This is a very, very last resort, especially if you have to reduce the memory size below the suggested size. Some robust applications can put up with undersize memory allocations, but many have trouble and crash or mess up documents. If you want to take a chance and need to see details on adjusting the allocation, see page 95.

CHAPTER 7

Printing and Fonts

Printing is putting your work on paper, as explained in the "Application Basics" section of Chapter 2. You want your printer to work well every time you print—no fuss, no muss. You choose **Print**, you click the Print button in the dialog box, and the printer prints; that's how easy it should be. On some computer systems, believe it or not, this is too much to ask. Users have to learn all kinds of fancy commands and code signals to send to the printer, just to print out their documents. It often takes three or four trips to the printer before the job comes out right. But on a good Mac system with a good printer, printing is a breeze. You just have to make sure a few things are set up right.

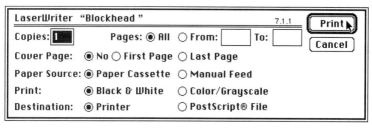

Illustration 7.1: Print dialog box

Checking Out the Printer

Get a good, reliable workhorse printer. Apple makes several great LaserWriters and a nice light-duty inkjet printer called the StyleWriter. Hewlett-Packard also makes a number of excellent laser printers and a hard-working inkjet printer called the

DeskWriter. Texas Instruments and GCC make excellent laser printers, too. Laser printers are more expensive than inkjet printers, but they are faster and they generally print out more dots per inch and clearer outlines of fine details.

Choose your printer carefully. Printer technology is always progressing, so you should shop around for the best deal, but avoid any new or cheap printer that does not have a strong reputation for reliability and compatibility with the Mac. Printers rely on drivers: software programs that interpret what the Mac tells them to print and actually put the images on the paper. If the driver for your printer isn't perfectly compatible with the system software on your Mac, printing can become a big hassle. If you install a new version of the system software on your Mac, you must get a new driver that is designed to work with the new system software. Now, Apple gives you new printer drivers for all Apple printers, free, when you buy new system software from them. Other good printer companies, like Hewlett-Packard, Texas Instruments, and GCC, make sure their printer drivers are perfectly in tune with the Mac system software. Some of them even give you free driver updates when the system software is updated. But some other printer companies are not so good about keeping their drivers up-to-date.

If you print lots of customized text documents, for desktop publishing perhaps, you will probably want to work with special PostScript fonts. For good results, these require the use of a high-power, true Adobe PostScript laser printer. For a discussion of PostScript and fonts in general, see "Different Fonts for Different Printers" on page 121.

Whatever kind of printer you buy, make sure it is connected properly to your Mac. Inkjet printers and the older ImageWriters can be connected by a serial cable to the printer port (the socket with the printer icon above it). Laser printers should be connected via AppleTalk cables; this costs more than the serial cable, but it makes for much faster printing.

Check the printer itself to make sure it is turned on and has paper in the tray. For details on setting up and connecting the printer, see its user manual. However, the easiest way to learn how to add paper to the paper tray is to get an experienced user to show you. Some printers, like most laser ones, have simple drawers that hold lots of paper. Other printers have spring-loaded paper feeders that are harder to fill.

Using the Chooser to Pick a Printer

The first time you use a printer that is connected to your Mac, you must select it in the Chooser, so your Mac's system software knows which printer to send things to. You have to do this even if you only have one printer connected. But once you have made this choice, it stays in effect until you change it; you can turn the Mac off, then start up, and it remembers your printer choice.

TO PICK YOUR PRINTER, first choose **Chooser** from the menu. The Chooser window opens, showing the icons of the different printers and network connections that are available. Choose your printer's icon. If you don't see an icon for your printer, you must install the driver for the printer. This is fairly simple. First find the icon for the driver of your printer on the Printing disk in your system software set or on the Installation disk you received with your printer. Then drag the icon to the System

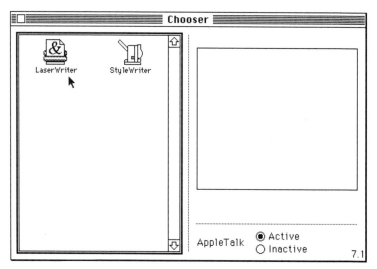

Illustration 7.2: The Chooser

Folder icon in your hard disk window. The Mac asks if you want the driver to go in the Extensions folder. Click OK.

If you are on a network, you may see a list of AppleTalk Zones under the printer icons. Find out which zone you should be using (ask your network administrator) and click the name of the zone.

When you have made your printer and zone choices, either a list of specific printer names appears in the list box on the right side of the Chooser window, or icons for your printer port and modem port appear (the modem port icon looks like a telephone). Click the name of the printer you want to use if you see a list of names; if there is only one printer in the list, it will be selected automatically. Click the printer icon if you see the printer and modem port icons. When the name of your printer or the printer port icon is selected, close the Chooser window. This finalizes your printer choice. The Mac doesn't give you any feedback to let you know that the choice is final (which seems odd to me), but when you print your first document you'll see that it comes out on the printer you chose.

If you ever need to use a different printer, first make sure it is connected properly to your Mac, then just open the Chooser, click on its icon, select its name, and close the Chooser. If you have any applications open when you change your printer choice, you have to choose **Page Setup** from the File menu of each application, then click OK; this prepares the application to send documents to the new printer.

Using the Print Dialog Box Before You Print

When you choose **Print** from the File menu of most applications, you see a dialog box more or less like the one in Illustration 7.1. You can use the options in it to change a number of things about the print job, depending on what you want.

COPIES

If you want to print more than one copy of the document, just enter the number you want.

PAGES

If you don't want to print all of the document, enter the numbers of the pages at the beginning and end of the part you want to print. If you don't enter a number in the To box, you'll get all the pages from the first number you list to the end of the document.

COVER PAGE

If you want the printer to add a sheet with your name on it, click one of the radio buttons to make the cover sheet come out either first or last. It's good to use cover sheets if you share the printer with lots of other users. You can tell the print jobs apart at a glance, so you can find your own quickly without being tempted to snoop through the others to find out who's printing what.

PAPER SOURCE

If you want to feed envelopes or other special paper into the printer one sheet at a time, or if the cassette or fanfold mechanism is broken, you can use the Manual Feed option and put paper into the printer. The Mac tells you when to feed the paper in as printing proceeds.

PRINT

If you have a color printer, you can click Color/Grayscale to print color or gray-shaded documents. Standard printers can only print black and white; they make shades by printing black dots on a white background.

DESTINATION

If you want to make a PostScript format file (that's a file with a whole mess of coded instructions that tell printers how to print out the image of the file) out of the document instead of printing a hard copy, choose the PostScript File option. The Mac writes the PostScript file on your current disk. It can take a long time (hours, if it's a complex graphic or a big text file with fancy fonts), so don't do it unless you really want a PostScript file or have a really fast Mac. For more on PostScript, see "Different Fonts for Different Printers" on page 121.

If you're like me, you will rarely need to mess with any of these options, other than maybe the Pages one (for when you only need to print part of a document and you want to save paper). In fact, if you do a lot of printing, you may get into a habit of starting the process by just hitting ⌘-P and then immediately pressing Return. The dialog box never appears. Now, that's the way I like printing to be. VERY simple.

Using the Page Setup Dialog Box

Sometimes you have to tell the printer to do special things, like print envelopes, or print an unusual font, or print sideways on the page. The **Page Setup** dialog box gives you options for all these things and more. Normally, you don't have to pay any attention to it. But when you have a special printing need, just choose **Page Setup** from the File menu, and you'll find these options:

```
LaserWriter Page Setup                    7.1.1        [ OK ]
Paper: ⦿ US Letter  ○ A4 Letter    ○ ┌──────────┐      [ Cancel ]
       ○ US Legal   ○ B5 Letter        │ Tabloid  ▼│
       Reduce or  [100]%          Printer Effects:    [ Options ]
       Enlarge:                   ⊠ Font Substitution?
       Orientation                ⊠ Text Smoothing?
       ┌──┐┌──┐                   ⊠ Graphics Smoothing?
       │↑👤││→🖥│                   ⊠ Faster Bitmap Printing?
       └──┘└──┘
```

Illustration 7.3: Page Setup dialog box for LaserWriter

PAPER

If you want to print on special-size paper or on envelopes, use these options. By the way, the actual sizes are: US Letter = 8.5" x 11"; US Legal = 8.5" x 14"; A4 Letter = 8.5" x 11.7"; B5 Letter = 7" x 10". In the Tabloid pop-up menu there are choices for extralarge paper and envelopes.

REDUCE OR ENLARGE

If you want to change the size of the text or images you are printing, increase or decrease the percentage from 100. At 100%, the material will print out as originally created.

ORIENTATION

If you want to print a section of a spreadsheet that is wider than it is tall, use the horizontal orientation, rather than the default portrait orientation. When you print something out in the horizontal or landscape orientation, people looking at it will hold the paper sideways.

PORTRAIT   LANDSCAPE   DISORIENTED

PRINTER EFFECTS

If you want the Mac to replace fonts that your printer can't print, check Font Substitutions. If you want jagged bit-mapped fonts to come out as nice as possible, click Text Smoothing. Choose Graphics Smoothing to rid graphics images of jagged edges. Choose Faster Bitmap Printing in order to print bitmap fonts more quickly on certain PostScript printers. The fonts may have a mild case of the "jaggies," but they print out fast.

OPTIONS

If you want to get special printing effects, like an upside-down image or precision bit-map printing, just click the Options button and check the checkbox you need; the little dog-cow creature in the dialog box shows you the effects of the image options.

Different Fonts for Different Printers

There's one thing you need to know about fonts, no matter which ones you use: in the old-fashioned printing press world, a font is just one set of characters in a given typeface, in only one size and style. For example, I work in Helvetica 12 point, plain style. An old-fashioned printer would have all the characters for that font in one specific box. But in the Mac world, when someone says font, they mean all the different sizes and styles for the given typeface. For example, the Helvetica font on my Mac includes all sizes from 9 to 24 point and all styles, including bold, italics, outline, and so on. Mac people refer to each of the different sizes and styles as a subset of the font. If you buy a Mac font, you should get all of the sizes and styles you need, all together. OK?

Now, there are lots of fonts out there in the Mac world, but I am content to use one serif font, Times, and one sans-serif font, Helvetica. As you can see, a serif font has the little doodads at the tips of the letters, and a sans-serif font has no doodads. Times is a good old serif font. Helvetica is a good old sans-serif font. They work fine for me. But many people find them boring.

To keep life interesting, fonts are changing all the time. Desktop publishing people are always looking for a newer and better font, so font designers can always sell a new font, and the big font companies like Adobe can really make a bundle by "improving" font technology and selling new "levels" of fonts. Sometimes other big companies, like Apple, get jealous of Adobe and bring out their own latest-greatest fonts. This can lead to actual font wars; Apple and Adobe pushing their fonts and printers at you, telling you why their stuff is better, and using a baffling mishmash of technical hype and subjective opinions.

You'd think that the competition would be good for you and your Mac. Sad to say, your Macintosh and the printers that work with it are always playing catch-up with the rapidly developing world of fonts. So if you want to use all the latest fonts, you have to get the very latest, fastest Mac with the greatest amount of RAM and storage possible, and you have to get a printer that is designed very specifically to print out the latest and greatest fonts. THEN you have to make sure all that font stuff will work OK with your Mac's system software.

It gets pretty complex and confusing, especially if you get used to one font set that works well with your old Mac, old printer, and old version of the system software, and then you upgrade one or more of those old things. The old stuff is often incompatible with the new (like I'm incompatible with day-glo running tights). Some new Adobe stuff works with some old Apple stuff but not new Apple stuff. Some new Apple stuff works fine with some new Adobe stuff, but not with any old Adobe stuff. Some of the new stuff doesn't work at all on old printers.

Sheesh. What a mess. And there's no evidence that it's going to get any more simple in the near future.

So what can you do? First thing, look at your Mac, your printer, your pocketbook, and your needs. Are you really set up and economically prepared to get into the big font chase? Do you really want to spend all the time, energy, and money it takes to keep up with font fashions? If you are a creative desktop publisher, or you are in charge of a whole group of desktop publishers, and you are publishing classy, fashionable ("slick" is what they call them) magazines or books, then you might say yes to the font fashion chase.

If you are like me, you'll see it as a worthless rat race. I say, get a printer that does what you want and does it reasonably fast, and use the standard fonts that work well on that printer. Skip all the complicated stuff in the rest of this section.

For those of you who want or need to know about fonts, here's a short introduction. There are two basic types of fonts;

the older bit-mapped ones and the newer outline ones. Among the outline fonts, there are PostScript fonts, often made by Adobe, and TrueType fonts, originally made by Apple. Bit-mapped fonts are drawn by plotting dots on the screen; typically, they have 72 dots per inch, like a traditional Mac screen. Outline fonts are drawn by means of complex mathematical formulas that describe the outlines of each letter.

If you have an old ImageWriter, use bit-mapped fonts like New York and Geneva. Fonts with city names are usually bit-mapped fonts. They map each dot or bit on the screen to a dot on paper. They look great on the screen and OK on paper as long as you have a resource file (a little file kept in the system folder; listed as part of the System file in system software versions before 7.1) for each size of the font you want to print in your system file. But if you want to print lots of different bit-mapped fonts in lots of sizes and styles, you tend to build up a huge System folder. This tends to bog down the Mac. And you can have problems if you try to print bit-mapped fonts in sizes for which you have no resources, using a PostScript printer that has to make a best guess of what it thinks that bit-mapped font should look like. Such best-guess printouts look very jagged; sometimes they aren't even legible.

More and more Mac users, especially those who do desktop publishing, work with laser printers or inkjet printers that use outline fonts. All you need is a single resource for an outline font in order to print any size of it perfectly, without ever having to make a best-guess printout. This is because outline fonts are just mathematical descriptions of how to create the outlines of the characters; once a printer has the outline drawn in a given size, it can fill in the outline instantly. PostScript outline fonts were the first ones to appear in the Mac desktop publishing world, and they are by far the most common.

PostScript is a page description language (a method of writing, in code, where you want ink and blank space to appear on a page) developed by Adobe for laser printing. Outline fonts were developed for PostScript printers, and they worked so well, it caused a revolution in publishing. So now there are thousands of PostScript fonts, and new ones coming out all the time. You can use these fonts on many different printers, but they work best with true PostScript printers that have licensed the Adobe interpreter to crank out their PostScript fonts. If you produce lots of documents with many different fonts that need to be printed out quickly, you should spend the time and money to buy a high-quality, true PostScript printer that can print at least eight pages a minute. Then make sure the latest system software is installed on every Mac that sends print jobs to your printer.

If you plan to use PostScript fonts, Install Adobe Type Manager (ATM); then you can clear most of the TrueType and bit-mapped fonts out of your System folder. All you have to do is leave one bit-mapped resource file for each PostScript font you use, so the font will appear on the screen. You'll wind up with a Mac that runs better, prints faster, and keeps your fonts in better order. For details on this undertaking, see a complete desktop publishing manual such as *Pagemaker 4, an Easy Desk Reference* by Robin Williams. It might also help to have an experienced desktop publisher (or font fanatic) help you get things set up and running smoothly. It ain't easy to set up a good PostScript font library on your Mac, but it makes life with fonts easier in the long run.

TrueType was developed by Apple as a simple alternative to PostScript outline fonts. TrueType fonts are adequate for most normal word-processing tasks. You can't do all the fancy fooling around with TrueType that you can do with PostScript, such as stretching and bending letters, but most of us don't need to do those things with our text, anyway. You don't have thousands of exotic fonts to choose from, especially if you are using a printer that is set up for PostScript printing, but you probably don't need thousands of exotic fonts. I'm willing to leave the font-bending and exotic fonts to graphic designers. If you want to use just a few fonts, such as the old standards like Times, Helvetica, and Symbol, you can use the TrueType fonts that come free with your system software, and you can print to an inexpensive inkjet printer like the StyleWriter or HP DeskWriter. No fuss, no muss, no font rat race. If you need to use PostScript outline fonts every once in awhile, you can use ATM with your inkjet printer, feed in high-quality paper, and make very nice, almost publication-quality printouts. The printing may take much longer than it does when you use TrueType fonts, but for occasional classy output, it's worth the trouble.

My main point in this whole discussion of fonts is that you don't need to worry much about them unless you are a very fashion-conscious desktop publisher. If you just want to print a couple of nice-looking fonts for your standard text documents, use the fonts that work best on your printer and don't bother with all the others.

CHAPTER 8

How Do I Get Outta Here?

This chapter tells you how to get out of 15 of the most common jams you can get into while using your Mac.

No matter what kind of jam you get into, the first thing you should do is stop, take a deep breath, and try to remember the last thing you did, or the last major change you made to your Mac, such as adding an extension or updating an application. Then try to solve your problem, using the appropriate section of this chapter. Make sure you try the easiest solution first. For example, if your Mac won't start up, make sure it is plugged into a socket with power before you reinstall the system software or hire a technician to replace the internal power supply. In each section, the easiest solution is always listed first.

The Mac Won't Start Up

This problem can manifest itself in a number of ways. Either nothing happens when you turn the switch on, or the Mac's screen stays black, or you see an unusual icon on the screen rather than the happy Mac icon, or you see the happy Mac and maybe the Welcome screen, but then the screen "freezes" before the desktop appears and lets you go to work. You may also hear odd chirping noises from the Mac, or a semi-musical scale of notes instead of a harmonious chord (if your Mac is one that normally plays a chord at startup, such as an LC or one of the Mac II models).

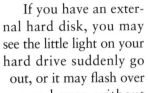

If you have an external hard disk, you may see the little light on your hard drive suddenly go out, or it may flash over and over, without anything happening on the Mac screen. You may hear unusual sounds from the hard drive, such as repeated growling noises instead of the normal ascending whir it makes as it starts up. Or the drive may be terribly silent.

Before you try anything else, turn off the power switch to the Mac and to your external hard drive, if you have one. Then make sure the power cords for both the Mac and hard drive are plugged into an outlet that has power. Plug a lamp into the outlet and turn the lamp on to make sure. If you have an external hard drive, make sure the cable that connects it to your Mac is firmly plugged into both the Mac and the hard drive, and that it is the correct cable. Then turn the hard drive on FIRST, wait for it to whir up to speed, and turn the Mac on. If it works, breathe a sigh of relief and go on your happy Mac way. If it still doesn't work, check the bold "If" statements beginning each of the following paragraphs, find the one that describes your problem, then do what it says to solve the problem.

IF YOUR SCREEN STAYS DARK, even though the disk drive whirred into action and you heard a beep or chord at startup, there is something wrong with the display. If you have a modular Mac with a separate monitor, make sure the monitor is plugged in and turned on; most of them have a little light that goes on.

No matter what model of Mac you have, if you are sure the monitor or screen is on, but it is still so dark you can't see things on the screen, or you can only make them out dimly, check the brightness control. On PowerBooks and on some older compact Macs and monitors, there is a brightness dial somewhere around the screen (on Mac Pluses it's under the left side of the Mac's "chin"; some monitors often have the dial on one side or the other). Adjust the dial until you can see the desktop clearly.

On some compact Macs such as the Classic, you have to adjust the brightness with a control panel. This is a pain. Get the room as dark as possible, then squint at the screen, pull down the menu, and choose **Control Panels.** When the window opens, squint some more and find the Brightness panel, the one with a little sun in it. Double-click it. When you

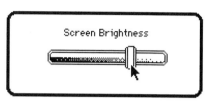

**Illustration 8.1:
Brightness slide bar**

see a slide bar as in Illustration 8.1, drag the slide bar to the right. Aah. That's better. If all your efforts to brighten the screen fail, take the Mac or the monitor to a qualified technician.

IF THE HAPPY MAC ICON DOESN'T APPEAR, your Mac can't get going with the system software that is available to it. Look at the icon that appears instead of the happy Mac; it tells you what the problem is. If you see a disk icon with an X, as in Illustration 8.2, it means there was a floppy disk in the floppy disk drive that didn't have the system software on it. The Mac spits this X disk out, then displays a disk icon with a ? in it while it looks for an internal or external disk drive with the system software.

If the ? disk icon doesn't go away, or flashes, your Mac is asking for a disk with the system software and not getting it. You have one of several problems.

Do you have an external hard disk? If so, the power cord to it or the cable connecting it to the Mac may not be plugged in right. Turn off the Mac and the hard drive, check the hard drive's

Illustration 8.2: ?, X, sad Mac icons

power cord and connecting cable, then turn the hard drive on and turn the Mac on.

Checking the plugs and cables doesn't help? If you have either an external or internal hard disk drive, the system software may not be installed on it, or there may be problems with the system software or driver software on the disk. If you have a Mac with 2 Mb of RAM and at least 8 Mb of free space on the hard disk, and you have had a lot of Mac experience, you can install the system software by using the floppy disks that Apple supplies and referring to a good full-size Mac manual, such as *The Macintosh Bible* or the *Macintosh Reference*. Otherwise, get help from a Mac hotshot or a qualified technician at a Mac shop; it's worth the trouble and/or expense to get your system software installed properly, and in the best configuration for your particular Mac. That way, it'll smile every time you turn it on, and you'll smile more, too.

Does the ? icon still flash with good system software on the hard drive? You have hard disk problems. First reinstall the driver software for the hard drive (using the installation instructions that came with the hard drive), then use a disk repair utility such as Norton Disk Doctor to check the hard drive for damage. If that doesn't fix the problem, zap the PRAM, as described in "If the PRAM is hosed," on page 131. If you do all that and the ? icon STILL persists, you have a problem with the hard drive. Take it and the Mac to a qualified repair shop.

IF YOU SEE A SAD MAC ICON, or hear a funny, nonmusical scale of notes instead of the musical chord at startup (on the SE, LC, and other Mac II family computers), something is seriously wrong with the disk that the system software is trying to run on. If you are starting with a startup floppy disk in the floppy drive, turn off the Mac, then wait a minute and turn it on with the mouse button held down. When the Mac spits out the faulty startup disk, insert a good one, such as the Install 1 disk you got from Apple with your system software on it. If the system software is on your hard drive, you have heavy problems with it or the driver software that runs it. First reinstall the driver software, using the instructions that came with the hard drive. Then check the hard drive's ID number and termination, as explained in "If the happy Mac icon goes on and off." Then use Norton Disk Doctor or some other good disk repair utility to fix any dents, dings, or damaged boot blocks on the disk. If those things don't help, you have hardware problems; take the Mac and the hard drive to a qualified repair shop.

IF THE HAPPY MAC ICON GOES ON AND OFF and nothing else happens, the disk has been damaged, the system software has been damaged, you have a SCSI device conflict, or the PRAM has been hosed. First use a disk repair utility, such as Norton Disk Doctor, to check the hard disk for problems, and let the utility fix them. Next, reinstall the system software with the help of an experienced Mac user, a qualified technician, or a full-size Mac manual such as *134*. Then, if you have an external SCSI (Small Computer Serial Interface) drive, check your SCSI ID number. It is a single digit number on a little dial or thumbwheel somewhere on the back of the hard drive case, and it must be set on a number from 1 to 6. If you have more than one SCSI device, make sure they all have different ID numbers, and that the hard drive with your system software on it (if it is an external drive) has the ID number 6. That will put the SCSI drive first in line when the Mac needs to use it. Finally, check your SCSI drive's manual to see if the drive needs a terminator; if it does and you haven't put one on, get one from an Apple dealer, plug it into the SCSI port on the hard drive, then plug the cable into the terminator. Some SCSI drives have a terminator built into them, so you don't need to add one. Also, keep in mind that if you have a chain of three or more SCSI devices, only the first and last ones in the chain need terminators.

If the external hard drive is terminated properly and has an ID number that is OK, the PRAM may need zapping; see "If The Pram Is Hosed," below.

IF THE PRAM IS HOSED (damaged) you have to zap it. This sounds like a big deal, but it isn't. On most Macs, all you have to do is start the computer with the System Tools disk or System Startup disk that came with your Mac. Then hold down the Option, Shift, and ⌘ keys, and choose **Control Panels** from the menu. A dialog box warns you that you are about to zap the PRAM.

Click Yes. When the Control Panels window reappears, close it. Choose **Restart** from the Special menu to restart the Mac. It spits out the floppy, then it should start on the hard disk. Zapping the PRAM puts any settings you have made with control panels back to their default settings. If you had custom settings, you have to reset them.

For those of you who have an older Mac Plus, you have to take the little battery out of the back of the Mac to zap the PRAM. Leave it out for an hour or so, then put it back in and start the Mac up again.

IF THE MAC HANGS OR YOU GET A SYSTEM ERROR MESSAGE during startup (the screen freezes or goes blank), there is probably a conflict between a control panel or extension (or INIT, as they used to be called) you just installed and some other part of the system software or some other control panel or extension. If you see a bomb message box, write down the ID (identification) number of the error, such as "02" in Illustration 8.3. You can give that number to any support people or technicians you talk to about your problem. They may tell you that you have problems with the hard disk or the system software, but since these problems are much less common, they are covered after the discussion of INIT conflicts.

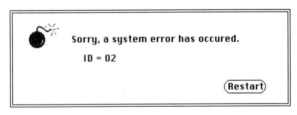

Illustration 8.3: System error bomb box

Did you recently install one or more control panels or extensions (INITS) on your Mac? You probably have a conflict. To resolve it, first turn off the Mac, then start it after inserting the System Tools disk you received with your system software, OR just hold down the Shift key while you start the Mac on the hard disk. When the desktop appears, open the System Folder, then open the Control Panels folder or the Extensions folder and remove the item or items you just installed. Drag them to another folder. I use "Disabled Control Panels" and "Disabled Extensions" folders. Restart the Mac on the hard disk (without the System Tools disk). If the problem still persists, take more of the extensions and/or control panels out of the their folders, until you find the culprit. Contact the manufacturer and find out if there is a later version of the offending INIT that does not conflict with others.

If the Mac hangs during startup even when you hold the Shift key down, the startup hard disk (the one with your system software on it, whether it is external or internal) has problems. Use a disk repair utility, such as Norton Disk Doctor, and check it out. If the SCSI driver for the startup hard disk is damaged, use the installation disk you got with the drive and the instructions in the drive's manual to reinstall the SCSI driver. Still no luck? There must be damage to the system software on the hard disk. Get help from a Mac hotshot or a qualified technician in reinstalling your system software on the hard disk.

IF THE HARD DISK ICON DOESN'T APPEAR ON THE DESKTOP at the end of the startup procedure, even though you have a hard disk connected to the Mac and turned on, your hard disk is having trouble talking to the brain (CPU) of your Mac. In fact, the Mac doesn't even recognize that the hard drive is there.

Do you have an internal hard drive with the system software on it? If so, first try turning the Mac off, waiting a minute or so, then turning the Mac on again.

Do you have an external hard drive? If so, first turn it and the Mac off, check the cable connections, and turn it and the Mac back on, hard drive first.

Did fixing the cable to your external drive and restarting bring the hard drive icon into view? If not, you've got some

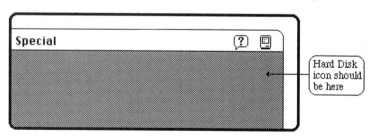

Illustration 8.4: Top of desktop with no hard disk icon

heavier problems. You may have damaged hard disk software, or a damaged desktop file, or an improperly terminated SCSI drive (external hard drive). First use a good disk repair utility, such as the Norton Disk Doctor, to check out the hard disk and fix any damage. Then try rebuilding the desktop file; all you have to do is choose **Restart** from the Special menu and hold down the ⌘ and Option keys as the Mac restarts. If the hard disk icon still does not appear, reinstall the driver software for your hard drive, using the instructions that came with the drive. Then check to make sure the drive has a usable ID number and is properly terminated, as described in "If the happy Mac icon goes on and off" on page 131. If all that doesn't help, the PRAM on your Mac must be hosed; see "If The PRAM Is Hosed" on page 131.

The Screen Freezes or the Mac Bombs

As you are working, the screen suddenly hangs, locks up, stops dead in its tracks; a bomb message box like the one in Illustration 8.3 may appear as the screen freezes, or it may freeze so fast the Mac has no time to put up a polite bomb. The Mac may even make a sort of rude burp noise, then go black, beep, and restart on you, or display squiggles, illegible text, and other garbage. Some people call all of these symptoms a system crash, although you rarely hear any actual crashing noises. Whatever you call the problem, it is easy for anyone to recognize, and chilling to all. You move the mouse and the pointer doesn't move. Sometimes the pointer actually moves, but if you try to click or double-click anything, nothing happens. Agh.

First, before you do anything else, take a deep breath, calm down, and try to save. Press ⌘-S. This is the keyboard shortcut for the **Save** command, and it may still work, even though the screen is frozen. It won't work if there is a bomb message on the screen. If there is a bomb message box, though, write down the ID number of the error, like "02" in Illustration 8.3. This can be very useful information to anybody you ask for assistance with your problem.

If there is no bomb message, and ⌘-S doesn't work, there is still something you can do. Unplug the keyboard and the mouse from the Mac, wait about a minute or two, then plug the keyboard and mouse back in. If the pointer comes to life and can select and open things, thank your lucky stars and go back to work; your frozen screen was caused by a simple static glitch in the cables for the keyboard and mouse, and you solved the problem by unplugging and replugging them.

If the screen is still frozen, write down any text you can see on it; if you haven't saved that text, you can at least copy it back into the document when you get things running again. Then make one last-ditch attempt to escape; press the ⌘, Option, and Escape keys all at once (on old Mac keyboards without Escape keys, press the ` key instead). If this gets you unstuck and out of the application you were in, save any work you have in other applications, quit them, and choose **Restart** from the Special menu to restart your Mac. Hold down the ⌘ and Option keys as the Mac restarts. This rebuilds the desktop file.

If your Mac restarts OK, the first thing to do is look in the Trash for a folder called "Rescued Items from (your hard disk's name)" Open the folder, drag any temp file you find in there out to your hard disk window, and try to open it with the application that made it. Most of the time, the thing will be empty, but sometimes the Mac manages to rescue some of your latest work before it crashes.

No luck after using the quick fixes above? Mac still not restarting as it should? Go on to the bold "If" that fits your problem and try the solutions given.

IF THE MAC RESTARTS OK, BUT YOU HAVE FURTHER PROBLEMS WITH THE APPLICATION, it is probably damaged; reinstall a fresh copy from the floppy disks you got when you bought the application.

IF THE MAC RESTARTS OK, BUT YOU HAVE MORE BOMBS AND SCREEN FREEZE-UPS, you may have two copies of the system software available to your Mac. In the Finder, choose **Find** from the File menu, or use some other file-finding utility such as Norton's Fast Find (in the menu if it is installed on your Mac) and search for "System." If you find two System files, remove not only the extra System file but any other extra system software that is in the same folder with it. Your Mac needs only one set of system software. It gets totally confused with two sets.

IF THE MAC BOMBS OR RESTARTS EVERY TIME YOU TRY TO OPEN A PAR-TICULAR DOCUMENT, that document is brain-damaged; it probably has a scrambled address or something, but the Mac can't handle it, at any rate. You can try to save the data in it. First just try to make a duplicate of it (choose **Duplicate** from the File menu in the Finder); if the duplicate works, throw the original in the trash and use the duplicate. If the duplicate still makes the Mac bomb, use a different but compatible application to open and translate the original, then reopen it with the original application, retranslating it back to something close to the original. Believe it or not, the file containing this very chapter turned into a mad bomber one day when I tried to open it with Microsoft Word. After some frustrating troubleshooting, I was able to save the text by opening and translating it with MacWrite II, then retranslating it back into Word. If none of these methods works, see a qualified expert at file retrieval; the data may be recoverable using special disk tools.

IF THE MAC CAN'T RESTART AFTER A CRASH, you may have any of a number of problems with your software or hardware. To find the problem, you have to try a few things out and do some diagnosing. First turn off the Mac and the hard drive if you have an external one. Check the power cords and the connector cable if you have an external SCSI drive connected to your Mac.

Next, try rebuilding the desktop, as explained above. Next, check for a SCSI ID number problem or improper SCSI drive termination, as explained in "If the happy Mac icon goes on and off" on page 131.

All of those things are OK and the Mac STILL can't get going? Drat. Start it from an emergency disk for a disk repair utility, such as Norton's Emergency disk. Then run the disk repair utility, such as Norton's Disk Doctor, and fix any problems that it finds. If that fails, the problem might be with the drivers for your hard drive. Use the instructions that came with your hard drive to reinstall the drivers.

No luck? You may be the victim of a virus; start the Mac with the emergency disk for a virus-protection program, such as Disinfectant, SAM (Symantec Anti-Virus for Macintosh), or Virex, and check for viruses, removing any that are found. If all of these attempts fail, the only possibilities left are defective system software or a hardware problem with the hard disk. Take the Mac and the hard drive to a qualified technician for help.

The Mac Doesn't Have Enough Memory

You try to do something mundane like open an application or a document, and you see a message box that tells you there isn't enough memory to do it. The simplest solution to the problem is usually to click the OK button in the message box, then quit one or more applications or DAs you are running at the time (just like the message in the box told you), then go back and try to do what you wanted. The following paragraphs give hints for more lasting solutions to memory shortage; for more details, see page 112.

IF YOU KNOW THERE WAS ENOUGH MEMORY TO DO WHAT YOU WANTED, but the Mac wouldn't do it, you may have fragmented the Mac's memory by opening and closing a number of applications and DAs of various sizes. The way to get the memory defragmented is to save your work in all open applications, close all of the applications, then restart the Mac. As a rule, it is best to start the applications that you use most and that use the most memory FIRST. Start little, rarely used applications LAST. This lowers the risk of fragmenting memory. Another thing that can take up memory in a sneaky way is the clipboard. If you have problems running out of memory and can't figure out why, it may be because you cut or copied something huge into the clipboard. Just copy a single character or dot to the clipboard, twice, to clean the big thing out of the clipboard and the hidden "Undo buffer" in the Mac's memory.

IF YOU OFTEN RUN OUT OF MEMORY IN A PARTICULAR APPLICATION, you can give it more memory. First quit the application, then find its icon in the Finder and select it. Then choose Get Info from the File menu, and increase the amount of the current size of memory allocated to the application. The current size number is in the lower right corner of the Info box. For example, if Word has a suggested size of 1,024K, you might in-crease the current size to 1,500K. The only problem with increasing the memory allocation for an application is that it means the Mac has less memory left to do other things, like open other applications. See the next paragraph.

Ilustration 8.5: Increasing memory allocation in Get Info

IF YOUR MAC OFTEN RUNS OUT OF MEMORY NO MATTER WHAT YOU ARE DOING WITH IT, you need to have a qualified technician install more RAM. If you want to run more than one application on System 7, you should have at least 4Mb of RAM. If you use memory-hogging applications, or work with large color graphics or huge spreadsheets, you may need much, much more. For more information see page 97.

IF YOU HAVE INSTALLED ALL THE RAM YOU CAN, AND YOU STILL RUN OUT OF MEMORY all the time, you should slim down the amount of memory your system software uses. Delete unused extensions and control panels, clean out any fonts and sounds you don't need, and turn off AppleTalk if you aren't using it. If all else fails, you can get a little more free RAM by reducing the size of the disk cache (RAM cache, to us old-timers). For details on all these memory-saving tricks and more, see "Reducing Memory Use" in Chapter 6.

The Printer Won't Print Your Document

This isn't supposed to happen with a Mac, but alas, sometimes it does.

Make sure the printer is plugged in, turned on, and loaded with the right kind of paper. Most printers have a little green light that tells you everything is ready for printing. If other lights are on or blinking, see the printer manual for details on getting the printer ready to go.

Then choose **Chooser** from the menu and make sure your printer is selected in the Chooser. Close the Chooser and choose **Page Setup…** from the File menu in your application. In the Page Setup dialog box, if there is a Destination choice (only a few Page Setup boxes show this choice), make sure the Destination is the Printer and not a PostScript file. PostScript files take forever to create, and they do NOT come out of the printer (see Chapter 7 for more on PostScript).

If you check all those things, and they are all OK, but the printer STILL does not print, you probably are trying to print a document with a font or illustration in it that your printer cannot handle. The most common problem is that you are trying to print a PostScript outline font on a printer that can't handle that font. Or you have an EPS (Encapsulated PostScript—or laser printing) or other special-format graphic, and the printer is gagging on the thing. Try to print the document one page at a time to pinpoint where the problem font or graphic is. Remove or change it when you find it.

If you are using a laser printer on a network, there may have been a bad signal that caused the printer to jam. Just turn off the printer, wait about ten seconds, then turn it back on. Wait for it to print out a startup page, which will indicate that it is ready to go back to work.

You Lost a Document in the Trash

Bah. You made a mistake. Two mistakes, in fact. You threw something in the trash that you didn't mean to. Then you emptied the trash. Don't take it too hard. You are human. To err is human. And besides, you can often recover the trashed document. If you have a file recovery utility, such as Norton Utilities' UnErase, Microcom 911 Utilities Complete Undelete, or CE Software's Rescue, you can dig the file out of the emptied trash. The Mac does not actually erase a trashed file until the space it is on is needed by a new file. So if you act soon, you can dig the file out and find it in good condition. If you don't drag the file out of the heap of emptied trash soon, however, it will decay. New files will start to use up the space it takes on the hard disk, and it may soon be so overwritten, it becomes useless.

So use the file recovery utility as soon as you realize your mistake. In most cases, all you have to do is open the utility, open the file list of trashed files, check the quality or "recoverability" of the file you want, then click the button that undeletes or unerases the file. I tell you, it's a grand feeling when you see it on the desktop again. If you want to make sure it really exists, just open the application that created it, then open the document and check the contents. Aaah. Such a relief!

One word of caution about recovering things from the Trash; don't try to recover applications. Even if the recovery utility lists an application as being in good or excellent condition, it still may not work properly. The only good way to bring back a trashed application is to reinstall it from the original floppy disks you got when you bought it.

You Have to Hunt for Files in Open and Save Dialog Boxes

This seems like an obscure problem, unless you face it often. The problem is that when you have opened an application, you have to navigate your way up and down your folder hierarchy from inside the application's Open dialog box in order to open a document, or you have to navigate in the same way when you save a newly created document for the first time. You get sick of opening that little pop-up menu under the title of the file list, going to the top of the folder hierarchy, then double-clicking your way down through the folders to the one with the document you want to open or the folder you want to save into. For more info on using this type of dialog box with a file list, see page 36.

There are two types of solutions. You can get one of a number of utilities that are designed to do an end run around the list boxes of the Open and Save dialog boxes, or you can figure out ways to avoid navigating in the dialog boxes at all.

If you want to try the utilities, a few of the better ones are ShortCut, Super Boomerang (of the Now Utilities), Findswell, and the Norton Utilities' Directory Assistance. Each has its own strengths, and some do searches for documents as well as open them, or search for a folder in which to save a new document. However, I find that some of them slow down the Open and Save procedures on my old Mac Plus, and others have conflicts with certain applications.

The avoiding solution can often be quicker; if you can find alternatives to navigating in the Open and Save dialog boxes, you don't need to use a utility that alters the boxes and slows down your Mac.

The simplest alternative to navigating in the Open dialog box is to go to the Finder (choose Finder from the Application menu), then find the file you want to open and double-click it. If you start in your hard disk window and open one of your main folders, then use a list view in that window to hunt your file, you can usually get to it quickly and painlessly. You can also go to the File menu and use **Find** or **Fast Find** (if you have installed it) to find your file. All you have to do is enter the name of the file or as much of it as you can remember, then click Find. If the search turns up a file with a similar name, just choose **Find Again** from the file menu until you locate the file you want to open. Then double-click it.

Another option for opening is to make an alias of a file that's in the folder with your most-used documents and put it into the menu. You can open that document first; then, if you need to open others, you'll find them listed instantly when the Open dialog box appears. For more info on aliases, see page 29. Another way to open that critical first document from the Finder without digging through the folder hierarchy is to put an alias in the hard disk window or on the desktop. If you use the same document day after day, you can put an alias of it in the Startup Items folder in your System Folder; that way, all you have to do is turn on the Mac and start work in your prime document and in the folder where you want to be for all your opening and saving.

Here's a nifty trick if you have a portable Mac and leave it plugged in between sessions. Just choose Sleep from the special menu instead of Shutdown; then all you have to do is click any key and the portable will light up right where you left off work.

If you work on documents in several folders, there is a utility you can use to go back to wherever you were when you quit work at the end of your previous session. The utility is HAM, by Microseeds. It not only reopens the documents you had open at the end of your last session, it puts a Recent Items folder in your menu, with a hierarchic menu that lists the names of a whole bunch of the documents you have opened recently. This is just as good as having an alias of the document's icon. You can reopen any document by choosing its name from the menu. I use HAM, and I hardly ever have to even see the inside of an Open dialog box.

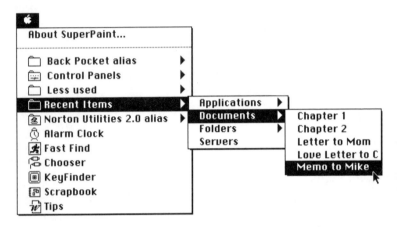

Illustration 8.6: The HAM Recent Items menu

Finally, there is a shortcut in the File menu of some applications, such as Microsoft Word and Excel; they list recently opened documents in the File menu; all you have to do is choose one and it opens; no fuss, no muss, no Open dialog box. Other applications are sure to follow suit.

You Can't Tell Where You Are in the Folder Hierarchy

This is embarrassing. You have opened a window, or maybe you used Find to find a file and open the window of the folder that contains it, but now you don't have a clue as to where the folder is in your folder hierarchy.

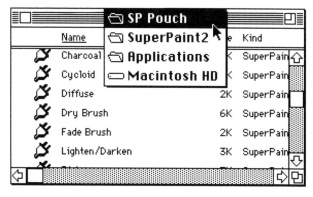

Illustration 8.7: Pop-up for hierarchy

The solution is simple. Just press the Option key and pull down the pop-up menu below the title of the window; the menu lists the levels of the hierarchy, right down to the hard disk or floppy disk. Keep in mind that the levels of the hierarchy are reversed, though; the top level, the disk, is at the bottom of the pop-up menu, and the folder you are viewing is at the top of the menu.

These folder hierarchy pop-up menus only exist for the titles of folder windows in the Finder. If you're looking at a docu-

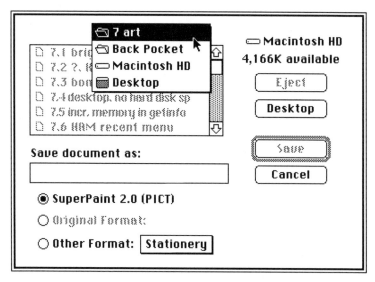

Illustration 8.8: Hierarchy pop-up in the Save di-box

ment window in an application, you can't open a pop-up menu under the title and see the folders that contain the document. But there's another way to find out where you are in the hierarchy; simply choose **Save As** from the File menu, then look at the pop-up menu under the title of the file list inside the Save dialog box. Click Cancel and you can go back to work. Slick, no?

A File or Folder is Lost

It happens to the best of us. You work on a document, save it, then go away and do something else, and when you come back to the folder where you thought you placed that document, it isn't there, and you have no idea where it is. Or maybe you just dragged the icon for a document or folder into a window with a crowded list or small icon view, and when you released the item, it scurried off somewhere, but you're not quite sure where.

Whatever the story, the feeling is the same; frustration. But the Mac gives you easy ways to find lost files and folders. If you want to open the window of the folder that contains your lost file or folder, use the **Find** command in the Finder's File menu. It gives you a little dialog box with a text field, where you fill in as much of the name of the file or folder as you can remember. Then you click the Find button, and in a moment or two, the window of the folder that contains your item appears, with the item selected. If there are several folders or files with similar names and your first search turns up a file you don't want, use the **Find Again...** command until you get the file you want.

If you want to look for items that were all modified after or before a certain date, or items of a certain size, or items in a certain folder, or items with other attributes, you can click the More Choices button in the Find dialog box, and use the pop-up menus in the larger dialog box that opens.

Some kinds of searches take much longer than others, and if you aren't very specific about what you're looking for, you may have to wait for a long search, or do a bunch of smaller searches before you turn up the item you are looking for. With these problems in mind, limit each search as much as possible. This is a bit hard to do, because the Find dialog box only lets you set one attribute at a time, and there are so many, many combinations of attributes that it takes forever to narrow the search down to a practical size.

If you want to do a quick and easy search for a file or folder, use a file-search utility, like Norton's Fast Find. You choose the utility from the menu, type in as much of the name as you can remember, then click the start button. In Fast Find, it's a button with a little running man in it. Fast Find gives you a list of all the files and/or folders that match the name you entered. Select an item in the list and Fast Find shows you its size, kind, dates, and location, instantly. If you want to open the item, just double-click it in the list.

If you want to move an item from its present folder to the desktop so that you can put it someplace else, just select it, then choose **Move to Desktop** from the Fast Find menu. If the item is a file, you can also view the data in it. For all items, you can open an extensive **Get Info** window that shows you all kinds of stuff, including a magnified view of the item's icon, which you can edit to make a new, custom icon. But the main power of a utility like Fast Find is that it can find your lost files, and do it quickly.

Two other file-search utilities, ShortCut and Findswell, can do the same sort of quick hunts from inside Open and Save dialog boxes. This can be nice for those times when you try to Save or Open something, but can't recall where it is or where it should go.

At another extreme, if you need to do lots of very complex searches, you can get a utility like DiskTop, which lets you simultaneously set a number of attributes for limiting a search. The only problem with this approach is that it may take you quite awhile to set up each search, and until you get good at the method, you may spend a lot of time finding things you didn't intend to look for. If you have a huge, complex Mac system or a network, and your job is finding lost files, it will definitely be worth the effort. But for us low-tech Mac users with limited storage space and nice tidy folder hierarchies, a simple utility like Fast Find is adequate.

To avoid digging down into folders to search for your applications and documents, you can make aliases for the ones you use most often (see page 29). Put the alias on the desktop, where you can get at it easily any time. I put aliases for my favorite applications in a row along the right side of the desktop, above the Trash icon.

If you have one or two documents you work on often, you can make an alias for each of them and put them on the desktop, too. Of course, if you make too many aliases and put them all on the desktop, it can get to be a cluttered mess. The trick is to limit your use of aliases to things you really need often. If you finish work on a document, just drag the outdated alias to the trash, so it doesn't clutter up the desktop.

You can also place an alias for an application or document in the menu so that you can open it from the menu without having to leave other applications and going to the Finder.

You Can't Find a Window for a Folder You Know Is Open

Your desktop is a mess, right? It can happen to anybody. I've got books stacked three high on my real-world desktop right now, and my wallet is under that mess, somewhere. On the Mac's desktop in the Finder, you may have ten windows, including a bunch of application document windows, spread all over the place. To find a buried window, you have to try a couple of things and just see which of them works.

First choose **Hide Others** from the Application menu (another way to do this is to hold down the Option key and click on the desktop as a way of leaving a document window and closing it on your way to the Finder). Next look in the currently active window and see if there is an icon for the folder that you want to look at. Even if the icon is grayed out, you can double-click it and its window will come to the front.

If you can't find the folder's icon, shrink or move the top one or two windows on the desktop and see if you can see at least a corner of the window you want. It only takes a second to click all the visible corners of windows and check them out.

If that fails, see if you can click the window for your hard disk, then double-click your way down through the open folder windows to the one you want. To keep this avenue open at all times, I put my hard disk window in the very upper left corner of my desktop, and I place ALL other windows, including documents, down and to the right a bit. Very few applications put their windows right up in the upper left corner of the screen, so it's easy to keep a little clicking space up there, where you can click your way directly to the hard disk icon at the top of your folder hierarchy. Another option is to keep all windows away from the upper right corner of the screen, so your hard disk icon, or some part of it, is always available for double-clicking.

If all of the above methods are of no help, you can hold down the Option key and click the close box in one of the folder windows; this closes all of the windows that are open. Then you can start at square one by opening the hard disk window and double-clicking your way down through the folders, or maybe change the hard disk window's view to "by Kind." Then, in the list view, just open and close folders to hunt around for the folder you want. But the list view for your hard disk can get so long that it is unwieldy. I find it easiest to keep the hard disk window in icon view, with only about ten folders in it; I put most of the windows for those ten folders in list views, so I can hunt quickly through each of them.

If you try all of the above methods and STILL can't find a folder to open its window, you have really LOST it. See the preceding section of this chapter for help in finding it.

The Mac Can't Find the Application to Open a Document

You double-click the icon for a document and you see a message box that looks like the one in Illustration 8.9. You know the application is on your Mac, but the Mac can't find it.

The solution is to open the application first, then open the document from inside the application, choosing **Open** from the Application's File menu. If you don't have the application that created the document, try the application that is the most similar to it. For example, if you have a MacPaint document, you can open SuperPaint first, then open the document from inside SuperPaint.

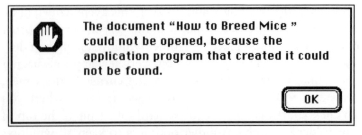

The document "How to Breed Mice" could not be opened, because the application program that created it could not be found.

OK

Illustration 8.9: Can't find application for document

The Mac Says a Disk is Unreadable; Should You Initialize It?

The answer is most often NO! So click the Eject button, unless you are sure the disk is either brand new and you want to initialize it so you can start using it, OR it is a used disk that comes from some other inferior kind of computer and you want to convert it to a Mac disk.

This disk is unreadable: Do you want to initialize it?

Eject   One-Sided   Two-Sided

Illustration 8.10: Initialize dialog box

If it is a floppy disk that you know you have used before, and you are sure it has documents or applications on it that you need, for heaven's sake, don't initialize it. Click Eject, right now, to spit the disk out of your Mac. If you initialize, you will erase all that valuable data. If, by some quirk of fate, you happen to click a button other than the Eject one (either an Initialize button, or a One-Sided or Two-Sided button), the Mac asks you if you really want to erase everything on that disk, and gives you a second chance to eject it. Click Eject to avoid disaster.

After you eject a disk that you know has data on it but that the Mac couldn't read, there are a couple of simple things you can do to try and make it readable again. Grab one corner of the floppy disk between two fingers and tap the edge of it briskly against your palm. This will shake any stray bits of dust off the disk and loosen up the door if it was sticky. Carefully grasp the part of the door that does not have the rectangular hole in it, and slide the door open and shut a couple of times. Don't breathe or blow dust or anything onto the disk while it is visible. Finally, turn the disk backside up, and put two fingertips on the metal hub of the disk, then rotate it a bit to make sure it isn't sticking when the drive tries to spin it. Insert the disk again.

If the Mac still thinks it is unreadable, it is probably damaged. You may be able to fix it by rebuilding the desktop file on it; hold down the ⌘ and Option keys and try once more to insert the disk; if a message box appears and asks if you want to rebuild the desktop file, click Yes. If you still get the "unreadable" message box, eject the disk, then use a disk repair utility, such as Norton Disk Doctor, to see if you can fix the damage. If that is to no avail, use a data recovery utility, such as Norton Volume Recover, to see if you can recover at least some of the files on the disk. After salvaging whatever you can from the disk, discard it. Do not initialize it and use it again; any disk that has failed once may fail again.

A Floppy Disk Is Stuck in the Disk Drive

You try to eject a floppy disk from a disk drive, and it doesn't spit out. You drag it to the trash, you use the **Put Away** command in the File menu, and still the thing just sits in there. The drive may make some almost human choking noises, but it can't spit the floppy out. Poor thing.

First try the keyboard command for ejecting a disk. Press ⌘-Shift-1 if the floppy is stuck in an internal drive, or ⌘-Shift-2 if it's in an external drive. Then try shutting down the Mac and turning it off and then on again. If the floppy is a startup disk, press the mouse button and hold it down while the Mac starts up. By the way, if you ever put a disk into the floppy drive and its icon doesn't show up on the desktop, try the keyboard shortcut above, then try restarting with the mouse button held down.

If the disk is still stuck, you can use a primitive but effective little tool to press the floppy drive's internal release button. The tool is a large (about 2-inch-long) paper clip. Straighten out one end of the paper clip and slide it straight into the tiny hole next to the floppy drive. When you feel the end hit the release button in there, push firmly but gently until the floppy pops loose. Check the floppy's door and hub for damage.

If the floppy does not pop loose, or comes only part way out of the drive, DO NOT try to yank it out with needlenose pliers or your teeth or something. You can destroy the drive mechanism. Take the Mac with the stuck floppy to a good shop and have a qualified technician extract it. And be gentle about pushing floppy disks into the drive from now on.

You Are Stuck in a Switch-Disk Nightmare

You keep seeing little message boxes that tell you to insert a different floppy disk, and the floppy that is in the Mac keeps spitting out every time Mac asks for another one. Most aggravating. To escape from this bad dream, press ⌘-. (period) once, or several times if it doesn't work at first. Sometimes it still goes on for a few rotations of disks, even after you smack it down with the ⌘-. command. When it does finally stop, try to recall what it was you did that got you into that nightmare (like ejecting a disk, leaving a ghost, and then trying to insert and eject a second disk). Don't EVER do that again.

Everything's Gone!

This can happen in one of two ways; everything in a window that you have been working on disappears, or, if you are using a version of the system software that is pre–System 7, you close a window and there is nothing on the desktop.

IF ALL YOUR WORK IN A WINDOW HAS DISAPPEARED, first try scrolling up and make sure it isn't just hidden from view because you accidentally scrolled down too much. If you don't find it that way, choose **Undo** from the Edit menu. If the stuff all reappears and is selected, you probably just hit a single key or the space bar and replaced all that selected stuff with a single character or a space. You have to be careful when you have lots of text or graphics selected. The Mac can delete a whole essay as easily as it can delete one word. See page 45 for more info on **Undo.**

IF YOU CAN'T SEE ANYTHING ON THE DESKTOP after closing a window, you are probably using system software previous to System 7. You see the blank background of the desktop with no windows, no icons, nothin' in sight. If you aren't using the MultiFinder, you won't even see an icon for your application at the right end of the menu bar. But you should be able to recognize the menu titles of the application you are in. To fill in the blank scenery, either open a document in the application or choose **Quit** from the File menu so the Finder's desktop appears with its icons and windows.

If you ever see a completely blank desktop in System 7, you have problems. Try restarting the Mac with the ⌘ and Option keys held down; click Yes when the dialog box asks if you want to rebuild the desktop. If that doesn't help, it's time to seek help from a qualified technician.

Help!

You tried one of the solutions to the problems above, and you are still stuck. Or you have a problem other than the ones listed.

The first place to go for more help is the Help balloons or the Help window that you can get in the Finder or in your application. The Finder gives you very helpful info and advice in the help balloons; just choose **Show Balloons** from the menu under the balloon-and-question-mark icon, then move the pointer to any icon or window on the desktop you need to know more about. If you have a Finder window open, such as the Get Info window for a file or folder, or the About This Macintosh window, you can point at specific lines of information in the window and learn more about them. When you have the info you need, choose **Hide Balloons** from the Help menu to make those insistent balloons go away.

Applications may or may not give you this much help with their balloons. But some have help screens that you can get to in the ⌘ menu or a Window or View menu. Just browse through the menus until you find a Help command and choose it. Once you are in the Help window, see if you can find an Index, then look up the topic you need help with. If you are stuck in the application, try pressing ⌘-Option-Escape (hold down both the ⌘ and Option keys, then press the Escape key; if you have an old Mac Plus keyboard without an Escape key, press ⌘-Option-. to do this escape). Then close all other applications, restart the Mac, start the application you got stuck in, and open its Help window.

The next place to look for help, after the Help balloons, is the documentation for the product you are having trouble with. If the Mac or the Finder has you stymied, see the Macintosh reference or user's manual that came with your Mac. There is a huge amount of information in this book. Take some time, use the index carefully, and do some patient hunting and studying; you will find answers to most questions you have about your Mac and its system software.

If you are stuck in an application, and the Help window is no help, read the application's documentation. Some are better than others. But even if the user's manual is hard to figure out, or it doesn't seem to address your problem, try to learn as much as you can about the feature you are having trouble with. You may find a way around your problem. You will at least know how to describe the problem in terms that the makers of the application will understand when you call their support department.

OK, let's say you have tried the Help window and the documentation, and you are still stuck. Agh. I'm sure you're feeling frustrated. I feel that way when I get stuck on the Mac, too. But don't give up. There is help as close as your phone.

CALLING SUPPORT is your last, and often best, option if you or your Mac is stuck and you can't figure out how to get unstuck. To find the support phone number, look first in your application's user manual. If you are having trouble with System 7, the number at Apple (at the time of publication of this book) is 800-767-2775. You have to pay a fee for Apple's support, but in my experience, you get plenty for your money; the people I have gotten support from are sharp, tuned in to the kinds of problems people have, and effective in helping solve those problems over the phone. Other applications may have free support, but you may have to call long distance (instead of calling an 800 number), so the phone call may be costly to you. Still, the help you get is often well worth the money.

To get the most for your money, if you make a long-distance or pay-by-the-minute phone call for support, get everything ready before you dial the support number:

1. Narrow down the problem and reproduce it if you can. If the Mac is frozen, so you can't reproduce the problem, at least try to recall and write down the actions you took that lead up to the problem. Also write down the name of any extensions or control panels you have recently added to your system software. New INITS are often the sources of problems.

2. Get your Mac running and be ready to reproduce the problem as you talk on the phone. If the screen is frozen, that's OK; the support person may be able to help you get it unfrozen.

3. Have your product registration number ready if you are calling an application's support department.

4. Jot down the version of the system software (both the System and the Finder if you can do **Get Info** on both of them) of your Mac and the version number of any application or utility that might be related to the problem. If you have done an upgrade or update to either the system software or the application, write that down, too.

5. Write down the critical memory info about your Mac, like how much RAM it has, how much is allocated to the application or utility that is having problems, and how much is allocated to RAM cache. If you are having trouble printing in the background (on a laser printer), find out how much RAM is allocated to the PrintMonitor, too. You have to select the PrintMonitor icon in the Extensions folder in your System folder, then choose **Get Info** from the file menu.

6. Write down a complete list of the extensions and control panels you have installed on your Mac. Even if you use an extension manager such as INITPicker to enable and disable them, and some were disabled when your problem occurred, write them all down. At the very least, have a name and version number for every one of those little icons that appeared across the bottom of your screen the last time you started up before having your problem.

There is one time when you should NOT call support. If you are having trouble with an application that you did not purchase legally, don't even dream of getting any help from the manufacturer. This is a secondary reason to avoid using pirated software; you can't call support, and you usually don't even have the documentation. The primary reason to avoid using pirated software, of course, is that it is a low-down, cheap thing to do to the creators and manufacturers of the software. If those people can't make any money selling good software, they're going to go out of business, and pretty soon there won't BE any good software. So pay for your applications, and then take advantage of the support they offer. The support you can get from Apple and applications companies like Microsoft, Aldus, and Claris is worth its weight in gold. Some of the smaller start-up software companies give great support, too. Microseeds, Baseline, and Intuit have all had excellent support since their early days.

GLOSSARY

ACCESS

To get at. To find and use. For example, it's hard to access a document if you can't remember which folder you put it in.

ACTIVATE

Click. For example, to activate a window, place the pointer anywhere in it and click. See page 24.

ACTIVE WINDOW

The window that is foremost on the desktop, ready for action; the title bar has horizontal lines in it. See page 22.

ADB See *Apple Desktop Bus.*

ALERT BOX

A framed area that appears on the Mac screen and gives you a warning or message. Read it, heed it, then click Stop or Continue (or OK or Cancel) to make it go away.

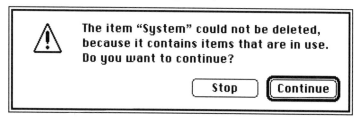

> ⚠️ The item "System" could not be deleted, because it contains items that are in use. Do you want to continue?
>
> [Stop] [[Continue]]

ALIAS

An icon that is a stand-in or substitute for the original icon of a document, folder, application, or disk. Has nothing to do with a nickname. You can use an alias as if it were the original. For example, you can have an alias of an application's icon on the desktop and double-click it to open the application. See page 29.

APPLE DESKTOP BUS (ADB)

Term used to describe sockets (ports) and cables for attaching the keyboard, mouse, and other control gismos like trackballs and graphics tablets to your Mac. See page 6.

APPLE KEY See *Command (⌘) key.*

APPLE (🍎) MENU

The menu at the far left end of the menu bar, under the small apple icon. You can put all kinds of good stuff in it. See page 50.

APPLETALK NETWORK

Apple's combination of cabling and software that you can use to hook up Macs, printers, and other peripherals.

APPLICATION

Software you use to do things on the Mac. Also called application program. See page 33.

APPLICATION MENU

The menu under the little icon at the far right end of the menu bar; lists the applications you are using and the Finder. See page 59.

ASCII

American Standard Code for Information Interchange; a code for the letters, numbers, and other characters on the Mac and most other computers.

ATM

Adobe Type Manager. A utility that can make PostScript outline fonts look better.

B

BACKGROUND

1. Where things can work without getting in your way. For example, you can print in the background and go on working on other things. 2. The color or pattern behind a graphic image.

BACKUP

A copy of a disk or file, which you can use if the original gets lost or damaged. See page 102.

BAUD

A unit of transmission speed: people now often say *bits per second,* or *bps,* more accurate terms.

BIT

Short for *binary digit*. The smallest unit of data a computer can use or store; either a 0 or a 1.

BIT-MAPPED FONTS

Fonts that are created by drawing many dots on the screen or printing them on paper. Each dot represents a bit; 0 is white, 1 is black.

BITS PER SECOND (BPS)

A unit of transmission speed. For example, some modems and faxes can send data at 2400 bps.

BOMB See *crash*.

BOOT

The nerd's jargon for *start up* when talking about a computer; a computer pulls itself into action by its own bootstraps, so to speak.

BUS

Electronic circuits that carry data from one part of the computer to another.

BUTTON

A push-button shape in a dialog box with a word in it. Click in the button to do what the word says. See pages 36-37.

BYTE

Eight bits. A single character of text is usually represented by eight bits.

CABLE

An insulated bunch of wires made into a single cord with connectors on the ends. See page 5.

CACHE See *disk cache*.

CDEV See *control panel*.

CENTRAL PROCESSING UNIT (CPU)

The Mac's brain. The chip that does the computations that make things happen on the Mac.

CHARACTER

A letter, number, punctuation mark, or symbol that you get by pressing a key or a combination of keys on the keyboard.

CHECKBOX

A little box next to an option or choice. 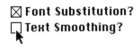 Click it to select or deselect the option or choice.

CHIP

A little piece of silicon with zillions of electronic circuits printed on it. See also *SIMM* and *central processing unit.*

CHOOSE

To pick a command in a menu by dragging down to it, then releasing the mouse button. Different from select, which means to highlight something by clicking it. See page 16.

CHOOSER

The desk accessory you use to pick which printer or network device you want to use. See page 117.

CLICK

To press and quickly release the mouse button when the pointer is on something. This activates, selects, or highlights the item. Some people say click on instead. See page 16.

CLIPBOARD

The temporary holding place in the Mac's memory for the last thing you cut or copied from a document. Things you paste come out of the clipboard and are copied into your document. See page 53.

CLOSE BOX

The little empty square in the upper left corner of any window; click in it and the window closes.

COMMAND (⌘) KEY

The key with the little propellor symbol; on most keyboards, the symbol is on the key, too. You hold this key down and press other keys to give commands. See page 22.

COMPRESS

To shrink files by digital wizardry, so they take up less room on your hard disk or floppy disks.

CONFIGURATION

The way things are set up; anything from options for an application, to the desktop pattern, to your whole computer system.

CONTROL PANELS (sometimes nicknamed *CDEVs*)

Little programs that put panels (like dialog boxes) on the screen so you can adjust sound, color, mouse speed, etc. See page 82.

COPY

1. To place a duplicate of selected text, graphics, or sound in the clipboard by choosing **Copy** in the Edit menu. See page 53.
2. To duplicate documents onto a different hard or floppy disk by dragging document icons to the disk icon. See page 32.

CPU See *central processing unit.*

CRASH

Stop working suddenly. Crashes do not hurt the Mac in most cases. See page 134.

CRT

Cathode Ray Tube. Nerd's jargon for the screen.

CURRENT STARTUP DISK

The disk that has the system software that you are using now. See page 69.

CURSOR

Name used for the pointer or insertion point on computers other than Macs. See page 14.

CUT

To remove selected text, graphics, or sounds and place them on the clipboard by choosing **Cut** from the Edit menu. See page 53.

DA See *desk accessory.*

DATA

Information, especially that which has been created or modified by an application.

DATABASE

Any collection of information organized into records that you can sort and search through easily for specific details.

DEFAULT

A value, command, or setting that the Mac assumes is best, unless you give it a different instruction. In dialog boxes, the default button always has a heavy double frame around it.

DEFRAGMENT

To rearrange the files on a hard disk so they are no longer divided up into little pieces; this makes them much easier for the Mac to use. See also *optimize.*

DELETE

To remove or erase items from a document. See page 45.

DESELECT

To un-select an icon or block of text or something; you usually just click on something else to deselect an item. See page 26.

DESK ACCESSORY (DA)

A mini-application such as the Alarm Clock or Scrapbook that is typically found in the Apple menu. See page 82.

DESKTOP

The working environment on the Mac—the menu bar and the gray area under it. See page 12.

DESKTOP PUBLISHING (DTP)

A setup for making publication-quality documents. For example, you can do desktop publishing with a Mac, a laser printer, and a page layout application.

DESTINATION

The file, folder, or disk that you are putting something on or into. See also *source*.

DEVICE

A piece of hardware that can connect to your Mac, such as a printer, hard disk drive, or scanner.

DIALOG BOX

A framed area that appears with a message or a request for a response from you, such as clicking checkboxes or typing numbers, then clicking an OK button. See page 36.

DIMMED

Grayed-out or disabled icon or choice in a menu or dialog box; you can't choose dimmed items. See page 19.

DISABLED

Not available; either dimmed or moved from the place where it is normally used by the Mac.

DISK

A flat, circular thing with a magnetic surface on which you can store information by saving or copying it. See page 90.

DISK CACHE (formerly called *RAM cache*)

A part of the Mac's RAM that is set aside to store often-used commands. See page 96.

DISK DRIVE

The device that holds and reads from or writes to a disk. You insert floppy disks in floppy disk drives. Most hard disk drives have the hard disk in there all the time.

DOCUMENT

What you make with your applications. Icons for them often give a hint of the application that made them. See page 26.

DOTS PER INCH (DPI)

A measure of how much detail a printer can print or a screen can show; the more dots per inch, the better the resolution, and the clearer the image.

DOUBLE-CLICK

To click on an icon or item twice in rapid succession, without moving the mouse. See page 16.

DOWNLOAD

What you do to a font to get it onto a printer from your Mac. See page 121. Also, what you do to get files from an information service.

DRAG

To place the pointer on something, hold the mouse button down, then move the mouse. The item moves as the mouse moves.

DRIVER

A file of software, usually in the System Folder, that lets the Mac direct the operation of a peripheral device. For example, a printer driver lets you send documents from your Mac to a printer to print them out. See page 117.

DTP See *desktop publishing*.

EJECT

What the Mac does to a floppy disk when you drag the disk's icon to the trash, or select the icon, then choose **Put Away** from the File menu. See page 57.

E

ELLIPSE COMMAND

A command in a menu that has three dots after it, such as **Open...** or **Save as...** in the File menu. See page 65.

E-MAIL

Electronic mail that you send from computer to computer, either over a network, or via a modem connected to telephone lines.

EPS

Encapsulated PostScript; a format used for graphics, typically publication-quality illustrations.

ERROR MESSAGE

A message that appears in an alert box on the screen to tell you of an error in an application's software or an error you have made using the Mac.

EXTENSION (SYSTEM EXTENSION)

A relatively small program that extends what your Mac system software can do. Kept in the Extensions folder in your System Folder. See page 88. See also *control panel*.

EXTERNAL HARD DRIVE

A hard disk drive that is connected to your Mac by a cable rather than being inside it (internal). Most are SCSI drives. See page 7.

F

FILE

A named, ordered collection of information stored on your Mac. Everything you use and make on the Mac is a file—applications, documents, utilities, drivers, extensions, control panels; all are files. See page 26.

FINDER

The program that runs the Mac's desktop and helps you find, open, copy, or move things shown on the desktop. You are "in" the Finder when you see the desktop. See page 12.

FIXED-SIZE FONT See *bit-mapped fonts*.

FLOPPY DISK

A 3 1/2-inch flexible plastic disk stored in a hard plastic case with a metal door. Stores 800K or 1.4MB of data. Other computers use 5-inch floppy disks in soft plastic cases. See page 30.

FLOPPY DISK DRIVE

A piece of hardware, usually inside your Mac, that reads from and writes to floppy disks.

FOLDER

An item on the desktop that can hold documents, applications, or other folders. On the Mac they have icons that look like manila folders. See page 27.

FONT

A complete set of characters in one type design. People in the printing world call this a single typeface, but in the Mac world, we call it a font. See page 121.

FORMAT

The arrangement and appearance of text (and sometimes graphics) on the page. For disk format, see *initialize*.

FRAGMENTED

Separated into several pieces. When your data and applications are fragmented, it can slow the Mac down. See pages 106 and 137.

FREEZE (*hang, gack, choke;* other unprintable terms also used)

What happens to the images on the Mac screen when the software stops working; the pointer stops moving and/or text does not appear when you type. See page 134.

GET INFO

A useful window full of information about any selected file or folder. The command to see it is in the File menu. See page 52.

G

GIGABYTE (GB)

1,024 megabytes. On a hard disk, enough storage to hold a small library's worth of text. "Gig" for short.

GRAYED See *dimmed*.

GROW BOX See *size box*.

HACKER

Person who messes about with the nitty gritty of computer hardware and software the way children mess about with toy boats in the bathtub.

H

HANG, HUNG See *freeze*.

HARD COPY

Information you have printed out on paper, as opposed to soft copy, which is stored on disk. See page 40.

HARD DISK

A nonflexible disk that is permanently sealed into a disk drive or a special cartridge for storing lots of data. See page 90.

HARDWARE

In the computer world, the machinery that makes up your system, such as your Mac, your printer, and other devices. See page 3.

HEAD

The part of a hard or floppy drive that reads from and writes to the disk.

HIERARCHICAL FILE SYSTEM

The Mac's way of organizing things; mainly files within folders and folders within folders. See page 75.

HIERARCHICAL MENU

A menu in which some of the items have little arrows on the right side, which let you open submenus to the side of the main menu. See page 50.

HIGH-DENSITY DISK

A floppy disk that holds about 1.4MB of data. You have to have a SuperDrive to use these disks. See page 30.

HIGHLIGHTED

Selected. Highlighted items have reversed video colors on the screen. See page 16.

HOT SPOT

The pixel that does the pointing on a pointer icon. For example, the hot spot on the arrow pointer is the tip of the arrow.

I-BEAM

A type of pointer that you use to place the insertion point I for entering and selecting text.

ICON

A little picture on the Mac screen that represents an object, a concept, or a message. See page 12.

IN

Small word with big meanings for Mac users. If you are "in" an application, it means you are using that software. If you are looking at the desktop, you are "in" the Finder. If you are looking at an error message box showing a bomb, you are "in" trouble. See page 12.

INFORMATION SERVICE

A computer or set of computers connected to telephone lines, so you can call in via your modem and read computer news and mail, do research, and download information.

INIT See *extension; control panel.*

INITIALIZE

To prepare or format a disk so that the Mac can write information on it and keep track of where the information is. The process has nothing to do with putting your initials on the disk. See page 31.

INKJET PRINTER

Type of printer that sprays tiny jets of ink to create text and graphics. The Apple StyleWriter and HP DeskJet are examples.

INSERTION POINT

The place in a text document where the next text you type will appear. Usually shown as a blinking vertical line. See page 43.

INSTALLER

A small application that comes on the same disk with some large applications. Double-click it to add the large application and its supplementary files to your Mac hard disk. See page 34.

INTERNAL DISK DRIVE

Either a hard disk drive or a floppy drive that is inside the Mac. You can't see an internal hard disk drive, but you can usually hear it whirring.

K See *kilobyte*.

K

KEYBOARD SHORTCUT

A combination of keys you press to give a command that is in a menu. For example, the shortcut for **Save** is usually ⌘-S.

KEY CAPS AND KEYFINDER

Desk accessories you can keep in your Apple menu to help you find they right keys to create a special character.

KILOBYTE (K)

1,024 bytes of data stored on a computer; about a half page of text.

LABEL

A word you can assign to a file or folder to help you categorize and prioritize it in the Finder.

L

LAN See *local area network*.

LANDSCAPE

Sideways, when speaking of how an image is printed on paper; you hold the paper so it is wider than tall.

LASER PRINTER

A printer that uses copierlike technology to print documents. Resolution is typically 300 or 600 dots per inch. See page 115.

LAUNCH

Jargon for open or start an application.

LIST BOX

A box with scroll bars inside a dialog box; usually lists the files and folders in the current folder. See page 37.

LOAD

Jargon for start up or open when talking about applications and documents.

LOCAL AREA NETWORK (LAN)

A group of computers, printers, and other peripherals connected together by cables so that the users can communicate with each other and share resources.

LOCK

To prevent files or disks from being changed or deleted. See pages 64 and 96.

M

MASTER COPY

Original copy of application software, or original (source) of a disk you want to copy. See page 32.

MB See *megabyte*.

MEGABYTE (MB)

1,024 kilobytes. On a hard disk, enough storage to hold a thick book's worth of text. "Meg" for short.

MEGAHERTZ (MHZ)

A million cycles per second. The unit used to measure the speed of computers; actually, it is only the rate of the CPU's clock. A slow old Mac Plus runs at a clock speed of 8 MHz; a Quadra 950 runs at 33 MHz.

MEMORY

The chips in the Mac that hold information ready for use. There is Read Only Memory (ROM) and Random Access Memory (RAM). See page 90.

MENU

A list of commands or choices, from which you pick one to take an action. On the Mac, you pull down menus from the top of the screen. See page 19.

MENU BAR

The row of menu titles across the top of your Mac screen; you pull down menus from the titles.

File	
New Folder	⌘N
Open	⌘O
Print	⌘P
Close Window	⌘W
Get Info	⌘I
Sharing...	
Duplicate	⌘D
Make Alias	
Put Away	⌘Y
Find...	⌘F
Find Again	⌘G
Page Setup...	
Print Window...	

MESSAGE BOX

A small dialog box containing a short note about something you have just done or are about to do, and with only one or two buttons to choose from.

MODEM

Short for modulator/demodulator. Device for sending and receiving data from one computer to another over telephone lines.

MODEM PORT

The socket on the back of your Mac that you plug your modem into.

MONITOR

The video display part of your computer. On Macs other than compacts and PowerBooks, the monitor is a separate unit, connected to the computer by a video cable. See page 4.

MOUSE

The gismo you move and click to move the pointer and select things on the Mac screen. The mouse button is the button you click and double-click on the mouse. See page 4.

NERD

Person who is so obsessed with computers that they can't relate with other people, and they like it that way.

NESTED FOLDER

A folder inside another folder. See page 75.

NETWORK

A collection of computers, printers, or other devices that are connected together so that they can communicate directly; you can send and receive e-mail and files over a network, and share a fast printer or a computer with large amounts of storage.

NOTE PAD

A desk accessory in your Apple menu for saving small blocks of text.

ON-LINE

1. Currently connected to your Mac and available for use.
2. Word describing information services you can connect to over phone lines with a modem, such as CompuServe or America Online.

OPEN

To make available or start up. In the case of an application, open means start up the thing. In the case of a folder, open means to open the folder's window so you can see what's inside. In the case of a document, open means to open the document's application and see the contents of the document so you can work on it. In the Finder, double-clicking opens icons for folders, documents, and applications. See page 16.

OPERATING SYSTEM

The software that runs any computer. In the Mac, the public part of the software is called the Finder; it's in your System Folder. There are also hidden parts of the software in the Mac's ROM.

OPTIMIZE

Similar to defragment when you're talking about a hard drive, but a little bit better; the files are defragmented and ordered logically.

OUTLINE FONT

A font that is created by a mathematical formula that draws the outline in any size, then fills it in. See page 124.

OUTPUT

What the CPU sends out to other devices, such as the screen, the speaker, the disk drives, a printer, a modem, or a network cable.

P

PAINT

Type of graphic and graphic application that involves bit-mapped images rather than object-oriented ones.

PALETTE

A set of possible tools, patterns, or colors for you to choose from when you are working in a graphics application.

PARK

What the hard disk drive does to its read-write heads to keep them away from the surface of the disk, so they can't damage it. See also *head*.

PASSWORD

A secret word you use to get access to something, like a file shared on a network, or your e-mail.

PASTE

To place the contents of the clipboard into your document. For example, to place cut or copied text at the insertion point, you choose **Paste** from the Edit menu. See page 54.

PERIPHERAL

Item you plug into the computer, such as a printer or hard drive. See page 7.

PICT (PICTURE)

Format for many object-oriented graphics, like MacDraw ones.

PIXEL

Short for picture element. One dot on your Mac screen. Each one is mapped to a bit in the Mac's memory; 0 is white, 1 is black.

PLOTTER

A peripheral device that allows you to draw with a pen instead of a mouse.

POINTER

The arrow that moves on the screen when you move the mouse in the Finder. It becomes a watch when the Mac is working on something, and a number of other things when you are working in different situations.

POP-UP MENU

A menu that appears in a shadowed box in a window or dialog box; use it as you use any pull-down menu. See page 39.

PORT

A socket for connecting things to your Mac. For example, the printer and modem ports on the back of your Mac are for connecting cables to printers, modems, and AppleTalk networks. See page 7.

POSTSCRIPT

A page-description language used by programmers to create images of text graphics for accurate printing at any size. Many laser printers use PostScript to make hard copies of documents.

PRAM

Parameter RAM; a little part of the Mac's RAM that is set aside to record control panel settings and some other housekeeping data. It does not get erased when you turn the Mac off.

PRINTER

A device you connect to your Mac to print paper or "hard" copies of documents. See page 115.

PRINTER PORT

The socket or port on the back of your Mac that you plug the printer and AppleTalk into. See page 116.

PROGRAM

A set of coded instructions for the computer. A piece of software. Applications are programs that you use as tools. See page 26.

PULL-DOWN MENU

The kind of menu in the menu bar. See page 19.

Q **QUIT**

To stop work in an application. Sometimes referred to as exit. The command to do it is in the File menu. See page 47.

R **RADIO BUTTON**

One of a group of small round buttons, only one of which can be selected at a time, like a push-button on a car radio.

RAM See *random access memory*.

RAM CACHE See *disk cache*.

RANDOM ACCESS MEMORY (RAM)

The part of the Mac's memory that stores information and instructions temporarily while you're working on it. See page 91.

READ

To transfer information from a disk into the Mac's memory.

READ ME

Name for document that comes with most new applications or utilities, telling you the latest info about the product.

READ ONLY MEMORY (ROM)

The part of the Mac's memory that holds programs written in by Apple; they never change. The Mac can only read them and use them for actions like opening and closing windows.

RESTART

To start the Mac again by choosing **Restart** from the Special menu in the Finder.

RETURN KEY

The key you press to move to a new line of text; also the keyboard shortcut for clicking the default (double-framed) button in a window. Referred to as the Enter key on some computers.

RGB MONITOR

A color monitor that uses separate signals for the colors red, green, and blue.

ROM See *Read Only Memory.*

RUN To start an application or process.

SAVE

To store something you have created; you can save to a hard or floppy disk. If you don't save your work, it just hangs out in the Mac's memory (RAM); so, if you turn the Mac off or if the power goes out before you save, your work disappears. So save often. See page 36.

SCANNER

Hardware that can transfer images and text into digital data that the Mac can work on.

SCRAPBOOK

A desk accessory for saving often-used graphics or blocks of text. See page 88.

SCREEN DUMP

Screen capture; a snapshot of what is on the screen, made when you press ⌘-Shift-3. The image is written to a file (Picture 1) that appears in the window of the currently active disk.

SCROLL BAR

Gray bar at the right edge and bottom of many windows. Use it to move backwards and forwards through a document. See page 23.

SCSI

Short for Small Computer System Interface, and pronounced "SKUH-zee." Refers to a connecting socket (port), a type of connecting cable, and all devices that connect to these things, such as external hard drives (called SCSI drives) and scanners. See page 7.

"SCUZZY" See *SCSI.*

SELECT

To click or drag across something with the pointer so that it becomes highlighted. See page 16.

SELECTION RECTANGLE

A dotted rectangle you can drag across icons in the Finder to select them.

SHIFT-CLICK

Way to add to or shorten a selection. If you select something, then move the pointer or insertion point beyond the end of the selection, hold down the Shift key, and click: new stuff is selected. See page 25.

SHIFT-DRAG

Way to select two separate groups of icons at once; drag across the first group to select it, then shift-drag across the second group.

SHUT DOWN

What you have to do before you turn off your Mac. You choose **Shut Down** from the Special menu in the Finder; the Mac does a sort of general housekeeping cleanup, then tells you it's safe to turn your Mac off or restart it.

SIMM

Short for Standard In-line Memory Module, a chip that is typically used for RAM in your Mac. See page 97.

SIZE BOX

A little box you drag diagonally to change a window's size. See page 23.

SLEEP

Option in the Special menu on PowerBooks that turns off the computer but retains current applications and documents in memory, so you can click any key and go right back to work.

SLIDE BAR

A graphic control used for adjusting things on a scale. It works much like a scroll bar.

SOFTWARE

Coded instructions that make the computer do things; usually in the form of applications or "programs."

SOURCE

The original version of a document, application, or disk from which you copy to a "target" or "destination" document or disk. See page 99.

SPREADSHEET

What an accountant's ledger looks like on a computer.

STARTUP DISK

A disk that has the system software the Mac needs to start up. Usually an internal hard disk.

STATIONERY

A document that serves as a template. Each time you open one, it makes a copy that you can work on and the original remains unchanged. See page 40.

STORAGE

Where you keep information and applications. Usually this is on your hard disk, with backup storage on floppy disks. See page 90.

SUBMENU

A menu that branches to the side of a main menu. See also *hierarchical menu*.

SUITCASE

A file that stores fonts or other resources such as sounds.

SUPERDRIVE

The floppy disk drive that comes in later model Macs, which can handle both 800K and high-density 1.4Mb floppy disks.

SUPPORT

What you need when something goes wrong on the Mac and you have no idea how to fix it. Most software companies and Apple itself have support departments you can call for help. See page 152.

SYSTEM DISK See *startup disk*.

SYSTEM EXTENSION See *extension*.

SYSTEM FILE

The file the Mac uses to start itself up and to provide information such as fonts or sounds that can be used at any time, by any application. You can't get at the startup program itself, but you can change the fonts and sounds in the system file. See page 121.

SYSTEM FOLDER

The folder that contains the system software than runs your Mac. It is the folder with a little Mac on it, usually found in your hard disk window. It is a crucial folder. Don't mess with it unless you are sure you know what you're doing.

SYSTEM SOFTWARE

The Mac's operating system. The programs that let you start and stop applications, give them the memory they need, and communicate with input and output devices like disk drives and printers. See page 10.

TARGET

This is the document or disk to which you copy something. See page 99.

TEACHTEXT

A small application that you get with your system software; it lets you read and write simple text documents and look at pictures.

TERMINATOR

A device used at each end of any chain of SCSI devices. See page 7.

TEXT

Words, especially when displayed on the screen so that you can work on them.

TEXT BOX

Blank space in a dialog box where you can enter words.

TEXT FILE

A file made up of ASCII characters only, without formatting.

TIFF

Tagged Image File Format; a graphic file format that is bit-mapped, but that can be resized and raised to very high resolutions.

TITLE BAR

| □ | Folder Title | □ |

The bar at the top of a window that shows the name of the window. When the window is active, horizontal lines appear in the title bar. See page 22.

TONER

Black powder that laser printers and photocopiers all use instead of ink.

TRACKBALL

Alternative to the mouse. It looks like a small pool ball in a little crater, with buttons on the sides. PowerBooks have them.

TRASH

Where you drag documents and applications you don't need any more. The trash can gets wide when it's full. See page 21.

TRUETYPE FONT

Apple's own outline font, made as an alternative to PostScript outline fonts. See page 124.

UNDER

Synonym for "while using" when talking about software.

UNDO

What you should do immediately after you make a mistake. Just choose **Undo** from the Edit menu.

UNLOCK

To change a setting on a file or disk so that you and others can change the data in that file or disk. See also *lock*.

UPS

Uninterruptible Power Supply. Get this if you can, especially if you live in an area where the electricity often goes out.

USER GROUP

A club of computer users who get together to share tips, information, and problems.

UTILITY

A relatively small application that does one or a few relatively simple functions.

VERSION

A number indicating the release of a piece of software. The larger the number, the later the release.

VIDEO MONITOR See *monitor*.

VIRTUAL MEMORY

Space on a hard disk that can be used as RAM.

VIRUS

A malicious program that spreads from Mac to Mac via floppy disks, modems, or networks. See page 136.

WINDOW

A framed area on the screen that shows you things like icons, text, or graphics. See page 22.

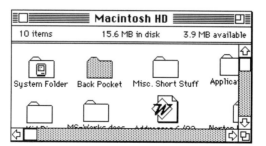

WORD WRAP

The way the Mac automatically starts a new line of text when the last word you entered won't fit on the line above.

WRITE

To transfer info from the Mac's memory to a disk drive, printer, or modem.

WYSIWYG

What You See Is What You Get. One of the crucial goals of the Mac desktop interface.

Z

ZONE

A part of a network. Networks can be divided into two or three zones, or many zones, depending on how big they are. See page 118.

ZOOM BOX

A little box in the upper right corner of many windows. Use it to change the size of the window quickly. See page 23.

INDEX

List views *(continued)*
  using, 79
  View menu overview, 54-56
Little Mac Book, The, 125
Loading. *See* Opening
Local area networks, 166
  See also Networks
Locked screen. *See* Freezes;
  Troubleshooting
Locking floppy disks, 34, 64, 166
Lu, Cary, 73

M

Mac Plus
  zapping the PRAM, 132
  See also Macintosh computers
Macintosh Basics tour, 13-14
Macintosh Bible, The, 10, 27,
  34, 70, 113, 130, 131
Macintosh computers
  checking the parts, 3-4
  heat and, 71
  moving, 67-68
  On/Off switch, 5, 9, 47-48
  practice using, 48
  restarting, 58
  setting up, 5-9
  shutting down, 47-48, 58,
    70, 172
  startup, 10-12, 127-34, 136-37
  where to keep this book, 1
  See also Hardware; *specific
    models or types*
Macintosh Reference, 10, 130
McQuilling, Carol, 81
MacTools, 89
Macworld magazine, 73
Make Alias command, 29, 52
Making. *See* Creating
Manual Feed option, 119
Master copy, 166
Mb, 166
Meg, 166
Megabyte, 166
Megahertz, 166
Memory, 90-98
  32-bit addressing, 97
  amount needed, 65-66
  for applications, 95-96, 114,
    137-38
  checking use, 50, 93-95, 112-13

control panel, 96-97
  defined, 166
  defragmenting, 113
  disk cache size, 96-97, 114, 138
  extension problems, 94-95
  freeing up, 62-63, 94-95, 97,
    112-14, 137-38
  installing more, 97-98, 138
  not enough available, 34, 63,
    94-95, 112, 137-38
  PRAM, 130, 131-32, 169
  RAM, 170
  Read Only Memory (ROM),
    92-93
  storage vs., 90-92
  system heap, 95
  virtual memory, 97, 109, 175
Menu bar, 166
Menus
  choosing commands, 19-20
  command key shortcuts, 22
  defined, 166
  ellipse commands, 65
  folder hierarchy pop-up menus,
    142-44
  grayed commands, 19-20, 49
  practice using, 48
  quick reference, 49-60
  viewing, 21-22
  See also specific menus by name
Message boxes, 167
MHz, 166
Mice. *See* Mouse
Microcom 911 Utilities, 139
Microphones, 8
Microseeds, 142, 154
Microsoft, 154
Microsoft Word, 45-46
MockPackage utilities, 90
Modems, 9, 167
Modular Macs, 1, 4
  See also Macintosh computers
Monitors
  brightness control, 83-84
  color, 8, 84
  defined, 167
  described, 4
  large-screen, 8
  plugging in, 5-6
  pointer at edge of screen, 15
  PowerBook screen, 73